Level Up! Egyptian Arabic Stories

Book 1

lingualism

ISBN: 978-1-962752-04-6

Written by Ahmad Al-Masri

Edited by Mohamed Mekki and Matthew Aldrich

Audio by Mohamed Shehata

website: www.lingualism.com

email: contact@lingualism.com

Table of Contents

Introduction ii

How to Use This Book iii

The Pigeon Tower 1

The School Songs 20

The Secret of the Koshari 37

Sara and the Cat 56

The Brides' Gifts 70

The Springs of Siwa 91

Introduction

Welcome to "Level Up!", a unique approach to reading in Egyptian Arabic. This series is designed specifically for adult learners, offering culturally authentic stories that explore Egyptian life, history, and traditions. Each book in the series contains six original stories, with every story presented in four versions corresponding to CEFR levels A1 through B2.

The innovative format of "Level Up!" emerged from learner feedback on our "One Thousand and One Nights" series, where readers who purchased both elementary and intermediate books found that reading the elementary version helped them build confidence and skills to tackle the intermediate version. This led us to develop a new approach: presenting all four versions of each story together, allowing learners to experience how complexity builds naturally while maintaining the same core narrative.

Why is this approach effective? When you read the A1 version of a story first, regardless of your current level, you build a strong foundation of basic vocabulary and story comprehension. As you progress through the versions, you'll recognize familiar elements while encountering new vocabulary and more complex structures gradually rather than feeling overwhelmed by them all at once.

Each story in this collection has been carefully crafted to reflect authentic Egyptian experiences and perspectives. From traditional pigeon-keeping to historical moments like the 1919 revolution, these stories provide not just language practice but also deep cultural insights. The adult-oriented themes ensure that the content remains engaging and relevant to mature learners.

Throughout the book, you'll find helpful features to support your learning journey. Before each story group, an Introduction provides cultural context, followed by Key Vocabulary that you'll encounter across the different versions. Every story has also been recorded by a professional Egyptian voice artist, with slower, clearer pronunciation for A1/A2 versions and more natural pacing for B1/B2.

How to Use This Book

The unique format of "Level Up!" has been carefully designed to support your learning journey. Here's how to make the most of its features:

Story Versions and Layout

Each story appears in four versions, with layouts specifically designed for different learning needs. All versions include voweling marks (tashkeel) on the Arabic text, using a simplified system that omits the fatha where it can be easily predicted, reducing visual clutter while maintaining readability.

A1 Version:

- Three-column format (Arabic script, phonemic transcription, English translation)
- The phonemic transcription helps beginners connect sounds to script
- Short, simple sentences with basic vocabulary

A2 Version:

- Two-column format (Arabic and English only)
- Phonemic transcription is removed to encourage direct reading of Arabic
- Slightly longer sentences with expanded vocabulary

B1 Version:

- Single-column format with English following each paragraph
- More complex sentence structures
- Quick reference to translation while maintaining focus on Arabic

B2 Version:

- Arabic text with English on following page
- Most complex structures and vocabulary
- Translation placement encourages independent reading

Reading Strategy

We recommend starting with the A1 version of each story, regardless of your current level. This approach helps you:

- Build confidence with the basic narrative
- Establish core vocabulary
- Recognize story elements that will appear in higher levels
- Progress naturally to more complex versions when ready

Vocabulary and Cultural Notes

- Before each story group, you'll find:
- An Introduction providing cultural context
- Key Vocabulary listing important words and expressions
- These sections help prepare you for all versions of the story

Audio Recordings

Each version has been recorded by a professional Egyptian voice artist:

- A1/A2 recordings are slower and clearer, with appropriate pauses
- B1/B2 recordings maintain clarity while using more natural pacing
- Use recordings to practice listening comprehension and pronunciation

- Listen while reading to reinforce learning

Remember, the goal is to read for pleasure and understanding. Don't feel pressured to move to a higher level version until you're comfortable. Each version offers valuable learning opportunities, and the familiar content helps you focus on new language features as they're introduced.

Visit www.lingualism.com/audio, where you can find the free accompanying audio to download or stream (at variable playback rates).

بُرْج الحمام

The Pigeon Tower

This story revolves around بُرْج الحمام *burg ilhamām*, a pigeon tower owned by عمّ مُصْطفى *3amm^ə muṣṭáfa* (Amm Mustafa). In Egyptian culture, عمّ *3amm* is a respectful way to address an older man–literally “uncle” but used more broadly in social contexts. The story introduces us to a clash between traditional pigeon-keeping and modern skepticism through the relationship between a grandfather and his grandson.

Key Vocabulary

- بُرْج الحمام (*burg al-hamam*) – pigeon tower, a traditional structure for keeping pigeons
- حمام (*hamām*) – pigeons
- شقْلباظ (*šaqlabāẓ*) – a specialized breed of Egyptian pigeons known for performing acrobatic movements in flight
- عبْسي (*3ábsi*) – a traditional Egyptian pigeon breed with distinctive black feathers
- زاجِل (*zāgil*) – carrier pigeon
- قرين (*qarīn*) – a spirit in Egyptian folklore believed to be a supernatural companion to humans that can cause mischief
- صقْر (*saʔr*) – falcon
- حفيد (*ɦafīd*) – grandson
- الدِّلْتا (*iddílta*) – the Nile Delta region where the story takes place
- طوب اللّبن (*ţūb illában*) – mud bricks, traditional building material
- غيطان (*ghiţān*) – fields, agricultural lands
- البِنايات الجِديدة (*ilbinayāt ilgidīda*) – new buildings/ construction, representing urbanization

A1

The Pigeon Tower	***burg ilɦamām***	**بُرْج الحمام**
Uncle Moustafa has a pigeon tower.	*3ammᵊ muṣṭáfa 3ándu búrgᵊ ɦamām.*	عمّ مُصْطفى عنْدُه بُرْج حمام.
The tower is big and beautiful.	*ilbúrgᵊ k(i)bīr wi gamīl.*	البُرْج كِبير و جميل.
It has many pigeons.	*fī ɦamām kitīr.*	فيه حمام كِتير.
Tarek is Uncle Moustafa's grandson.	*ṭāri? ɦafīd 3ammᵊ muṣṭáfa.*	طارِق حفيد عمّ مُصْطفى.
He is fifteen years old.	*3úmru xamastāšar sána.*	عُمْرُه خمسْتاشر سنة.
He doesn't like pigeons.	*miš biyɦíbb ilɦamām.*	مِش بِيْحِبّ الحمام.
One day:	*fi yōm:*	في يوْم:
– A pigeon flew away	*– ɦamāma ṭārit bi3īd*	- حمامة طارِت بِعيد
– Then another pigeon	*– wi ba3dēn ɦamāma tánya*	- و بعْديْن حمامة تانْيَة

– Then a third pigeon	*– wi ba3dēn ɧamāma tálta*	- و بعْديْن حمامة تالْتة
Uncle Moustafa is sad.	*3ammᵊ muşţáfa za3lān.*	عمّ مُصْطفى زعْلان.
He said, "It's the qareen!"	*ʔāl: "da -lqarīn!"*	قال: "ده القرين!"
Tarek doesn't believe.	*ţāriʔ miš mişáddaʔ.*	طارِق مِش مِصدّق.
Tarek watched the tower:	*ţāriʔ rāʔib ilburg:*	طارِق راقِب البُرْج:
– In the morning	*– fi -şşubɧ*	- في الصُّبْح
– At noon	*– fi -ḍḍuhr*	- في الضُّهْر
– In the evening	*– fi -ilmáɣrib*	- في المغْرِب
And he saw a big falcon!	*wi šāf şaʔrᵊ k(i)bīr!*	و شاف صقْر كِبير!
The falcon is hungry.	*işşáʔrᵊ ga3ān.*	الصّقْر جعان.
Its home is gone because of new buildings.	*bētu rāɧ bi-sábab ilbinayāt ilgidīda.*	بيْتُه راح بِسبب البِنايات الجِديدة.
Tarek and his friends helped the falcon:	*ţāriʔ wi ʔaşɧābu sá3du -şşaʔr:*	طارِق و أصْحابُه ساعْدوا الصّقْر:
– They made it a home	*– 3amalūlu bēt*	- عملولُه بيْت
– In the mountain	*– fi -lgábal*	- في الجبل

– Far from the pigeons	– bi3īd 3an ilḫamām	- بِعيد عن الحمام
Now:	dilwaʔtī:	دِلْوَقْتي:
– The pigeons are happy	– ilḫamām mabsūṭ	- الحمام مبْسوط
– The falcon is happy	– iṣṣáʔrᵊ mabsūṭ	- الصّقْر مبْسوط
– Uncle Moustafa is happy	– 3ammᵊ muṣṭáfa mabsūṭ	- عمّ مُصْطفى مبْسوط
– And Tarek loves pigeons	– wi ṭāriʔ biyḫíbb ilḫamām	- و طارِق بِيْحِبّ الحمام

The Pigeon Tower	بُرْج الحمام
In a small Delta village, Uncle Moustafa has a big pigeon tower. This tower has been in his family since his grandfather's time. Every day, he goes up early to feed the pigeons and let them fly.	في قرْيَة صُغيّرة في الدِّلْتا، عمّ مُصْطفى عنْدُه بُرْج حمام كِبير. البُرْج ده عنْدُه مِن أيّام جِدُّه. كُلّ يوْم، بِيِطْلع الصُّبْح يِأكِّل الحمام و يِطيّرُه.
His grandson Tarek is fifteen years old. He's not interested in pigeons at all. He always says, "Grandpa, it's 2024! Nobody raises pigeons nowadays!"	حفيدُه طارِق عنْدُه خمسْتاشر سنة. مِش مُهْتمّ بِالْحمام خالِص. دايْماً بِيْقول: "يا جِدّو، إحْنا في ٢٠٢٤! محدِّش بِيْربّي حمام دِلْوَقْتي!"
One day, Uncle Moustafa noticed that pigeons were disappearing. Every two or three days, a pigeon would vanish.	في يوْم، عمّ مُصْطفى لاحِظ إنّ الحمام بِيِخْتِفي. كُلّ يوْميْن تلاتة، حمامة تِخْتِفي.
"Tarek, something strange is happening!"	"يا طارِق، في حاجة غريبة بِتِحْصل!"
"Maybe it's cats, Grandpa?"	"يِمْكِن القُطط يا جِدّو؟"
"No, I know about cats. This is something else... this is the work of the qareen!"	"لأ، أنا عارِف القُطط. دي حاجة تانْيَة... دي شُغْل القرين!"
"Qareen?!" Tarek laughed. "Grandpa, the qareen is just superstition!"	"قرين؟!" ضِحِك طارِق. "يا جِدّو، القرين ده خُرافات!"

Uncle Moustafa told him, "Your great-grandfather saw the qareen. It used to take pigeons just like this!"	عمّ مُصْطفى حكى: "جِدّك الكِبير شاف القرين. كان بِياخُد الحمام زيّ كِده!"
Tarek doesn't believe it but decided to help his grandfather. Every day, he watched the tower. And one day, he saw something in the sky.	طارِق مِش مِصدّق، بسّ قرّر يِساعِد جِدُّه. كُلّ يوْم، قعد يِراقِب البُرْج. و في يوْم، شاف حاجة في السّما.
A big bird... but not a qareen. It's a falcon! The falcon was flying in the new area they're building near the village.	طير كِبير... بسّ مِش قرين. ده صقْر! الصّقْر بِيْطير في المنْطِقة الجِديدة اللي بِيِبْنوها قُريِّب مِن القرْيَة.
Tarek researched the subject on the internet. The falcons are coming to the area because the new buildings took their lands.	طارِق دوّر على النِّت عن الموْضوع ده. الصُّقور بِتيجي لِلْمنْطِقة عشان البِنايات الجِديدة خدِت أراضيهُم.
"Look, Grandpa! The falcons need a place to live. The new buildings took their home!"	"بُصّ يا جِدّو! الصُّقور مِحْتاجة مكان يِعيشوا فيه. البِنايات الجِديدة خدِت بِيْتْهُم!"
Uncle Moustafa understood. "Well, what's the solution, Tarek?"	عمّ مُصْطفى فِهِم. "طيب، و أيْه الحلّ يا طارِق؟"
Tarek thought and said, "I have an idea!"	طارِق فكّر و قال: "عنْدي فِكْرة!"

Tarek went with his friends and made small houses for the falcons in the nearby mountain. The falcons found a place to live, and left Uncle Moustafa’s pigeons in peace.	راح طارِق معَ صُحابُه، عملوا بِيوت صُغيّرة لِلصُّقور في الجبل القُريِّب. الصُّقور لقِت مكان تِعيش فيه، و سابِت حمام عمّ مُصْطفى في سلام.
Now, Tarek goes up to the tower with his grandfather every day. He learns everything about pigeons from him:	دِلْوَقْتي، طارِق بِيِطْلع كُلّ يوْم معَ جِدُّه البُرْج. بِيِتْعلِّم مِنُّه كُلّ حاجة عن الحمام:
– How to choose good pigeons	- إزّاي يِخْتار الحمام الكُوَيِّس
– When to fly each type	- إمْتى يِطيّر كُلّ نوْع
– How to recognize a sick pigeon	- إزّاي يِعْرف الحمامة المريضة
And one day he told his grandfather, “You know what, Grandpa? Pigeons turned out to be nice... not like what I thought!”	و في يوْم قال لِجِدُّه: ”عارِف يا جِدّو؟ الحمام طِلِع حِلْو... بسّ مِش زيّ ما كُنْت فاكِر!“
Uncle Moustafa laughed, “And you turned out smarter than your grandfather... you solved the problem without believing in the qareen!”	عمّ مُصْطفى ضِحِك: ”وكمان طِلِعْت أذْكى مِن جِدّك... حلّيْت المُشْكِلة مِن غيْر ما تِصدّق في القرين!“

بُرْج الحمام

The Pigeon Tower

في قرْيَة صُغيّرة مِن قُرى الدِّلْتا، حيْث الغيطان الخضْرا بِتِمْتِدّ على قدّ ما العيْن تِقْدر تِشوف، هتْلاقي بُرْج حمام عمّ مُصْطفى اللي أعْلى مِن أيّ بُرْج تاني مَوْجود. البُرْج ده مِش مُجرّد مبْنى - ده تاريخ عيْلة كامْلة. جِدّ عمّ مُصْطفى بناه بإيدُه مِن الطّوب اللّبن، و أبوه زوِّد عليْه دوْر، و دِلْوَقْتي عمّ مُصْطفى بِيْحافِظ على المَوْضوع ده.

In a small village in the Delta, where the green fields stretch as far as the eye can see, stands Uncle Moustafa's pigeon tower, taller than any other tower around. This tower isn't just a building – it's an entire family's history. Uncle Moustafa's grandfather built it with his own hands from mud bricks, his father added another floor, and now Uncle Moustafa maintains this tradition.

كُلّ يوْم، قبْل ما الشّمْس تِطْلع، عمّ مُصْطفى بِيِطْلع السّلالِم الضّيّقة لِلْبُرْج. بِيِفْتح الشّبابيك الخشب، و بِيِسْمع صوْت الحمام بِيْسلِّم عليْه. عنْدُه أنْواع كِتير: الزّاجِل الأبْيَض، و الشّقْلباظ اللي بِيِعْمِل حركات في الهَوا، و العبْسي اللي ريشُه إسْوِد لامِع.

Every day, before sunrise, Uncle Moustafa climbs the narrow stairs to the tower. He opens the wooden windows and hears the pigeons greeting him. He has many types: the white carrier pigeons, the acrobatic Shaqlabaz that performs tricks in the air, and the Absi with its shiny black feathers.

حفيدُه طارِق، طالِب في أولى ثانَوي، شايِف إنّ ترْبيةْ الحمام دي حاجة قديمة. "يا جِدّو، النّاس دِلْوَقْتي عنْدها موبايْلات و إنْترْنت. محدِّش بِيِبْعت رسايِل معَ الحمام زيّ زمان!"

His grandson Tarek, a first-year secondary school student, sees pigeon-keeping as something outdated. "Grandpa, people nowadays have mobile phones and internet. Nobody sends messages with pigeons like in the old days!"

عمّ مُصْطفى بِيِبْتِسِم: "الحمام مِش لِلرّسايِل بسّ يا طارِق. دي فِطْرة و صنْعة. كُلّ طيْر فيهُم لُه شخْصية."

Uncle Moustafa smiles, "Pigeons aren't just for messages, Tarek. It's instinct and craftsmanship. Each bird has its own personality."

المُشْكِلة بدأِت لمّا الحمام بدأ يِخْتِفي. الأوِّل، اِخْتفِت حمامة بيْضا مِن أحْسن الزّاجِل. و بعْديْن، كُلّ كام يوْم، حمامة تانْيَة تِضيع. عمّ مُصْطفى قِلِق، و بدأ يِحُطّ علامات على قدم كُلّ حمامة عشان يِعْرف مين اللي بِيِخْتِفي.

The problem started when pigeons began disappearing. First, a white pigeon vanished, one of the best carriers. Then, every few days, another pigeon would disappear. Uncle Moustafa grew worried and started putting marks on each pigeon's foot to track which ones were disappearing.

"أكيد ده شُغْل القرين!" قال عمّ مُصْطفى بِثِقّة. "أبويا حكالي إنّ القرين ظهرْلُه هِنا في البُرْج ده. كان بِياخُد الحمام الكُوَيِّس بسّ."

"This must be the work of the qareen!" said Uncle Moustafa confidently. "My father told me the qareen appeared to him here in this tower. It would only take the good pigeons."

طارِق، اللي مِتْعوِّد يِدوّر على تفْسير عِلْمي لِكُلّ حاجة، مكانْش مُقْتنع. "يا جِدّو، لازِم يِكون فيه سبب منْطقي. مُمْكِن أقْعُد في البُرْج أراقِب؟"

Tarek, who was used to looking for scientific explanations for everything, wasn't convinced. "Grandpa, there must be a logical reason. Can I stay in the tower and watch?"

عمّ مُصْطفى وافِق، و طارِق بدأ مُهِمِّتُه. جاب الكاميرا بِتاعْتُه، و لابْتوْب قديم، و قعد يِسجِّل كُلّ حاجة بِتِحْصل حَواليْن البُرْج. لاحِظ إنّ الحمام بِيِتْوَتّر في أَوْقات مُعيّنة، و بِيِخْتِفي دايْماً في نفْس الوَقْت مِن اليوْم.

Uncle Moustafa agreed, and Tarek began his mission. He brought his camera, an old laptop, and started recording everything that happened around the tower. He noticed that the pigeons would get nervous at certain times and would always disappear at the same time of day.

في يوْم، و هُوَّ قاعِد في البُرْج بِيْراقِب، شاف حاجة كِبيرة بِتْطير في السّما. صقْر جميل، بُنّي مِحمِرّ، بِيْحوم فوْق البُرْج. طارِق صوّر الصّقْر و بدأ يِدوّر في الإنْترْنِت. اِكْتشف إنّ ده صقْر حُرّ، مِن النّوْع اللي كان عايِش في المنْطِقة مِن زمان.

One day, while watching from the tower, he saw something large flying in the sky. A beautiful falcon, reddish-brown, circling above the tower. Tarek photographed the falcon and started searching the internet. He discovered it was a free falcon, a species that had lived in the area for ages.

"بُصّ يا جِدّو!" قال طارِق و هُوَّ بِيْوَرّي جِدُّه الصُّوَر. "الصُّقور دي كانِت عايْشة في الأراضي اللي بِيِبْنوا عليْها المدينة الجِديدة. لمّا خدوا أرْضُهُم، بدأوا يِدوّروا على أكْل في حِتت تانْيَة."

"Look, Grandpa!" said Tarek, showing his grandfather the photos. "These falcons used to live in the lands where they're building the new city. When they took their land, they started looking for food in other places."

عمّ مُصْطفى بصّ لِلصُّوَر بِاهْتِمام: "برْضُه القرين... بسّ المرّة دي شكْله اِتْغيّر!"

Uncle Moustafa looked at the photos with interest. "Still the qareen... but this time it changed its form!"

طارِق فكّر في حلّ. معَ صُحابُه في المدْرسة، بدأوا يِعْمِلوا بحْث عن الصُّقور المصْرية. عِرْفوا إنّها بِتِحْتاج أماكِن عالْيَة تِبْني فيها أعْشاشْها. و في الجبل القُريِّب مِن القرْيَة، لقواأماكِن مُناسْبة.

Tarek thought of a solution. With his school friends, they began researching Egyptian falcons. They learned that falcons need high places to build their nests. And in the mountain near the village, they found suitable locations.

بِمُساعدِةْ مُدرِّس العُلوم، عملوا بِيوت خشب صُغيّرة لِلصُّقور، و حطّوها في الجبل. حطّوا جُوّاها أكْل لِلصُّقور، و معَ الوَقْت، الصُّقور بدأِت تِسْتقِرّ هِناك.

With help from their science teacher, they made small wooden houses for the falcons and placed them in the mountain. They put food inside for the falcons, and over time, the falcons began to settle there.

الحمام رِجِع يِطير في أمان، و الصُّقور لقِت بيْت جِديد. طارِق بدأ يِطْلع معَ جِدُّه البُرْج كُلّ يوْم، مِش عشان يُحْرُس الحمام بسّ، لكِن عشان اِكْتشف إنّ فيه حاجات حِلْوَة في التّقاليد القديمة.

The pigeons returned to flying safely, and the falcons found a new home. Tarek started going up to the tower with his grandfather every day, not just to guard the pigeons, but because he discovered there was beauty in old traditions.

"تِعْرف يا جِدّو؟" طارِق قال و هُوَّ بِيْراقِب حمامة شقْلباظ بِتِعْمِل حركات في الهَوا. "يِمْكِن مفيش قرين، بسّ فيه سِحْر برْضُه في الحمام ده!"

"You know, Grandpa?" said Tarek while watching a Shaqlabaz pigeon performing tricks in the air. "Maybe there's no qareen, but there's still magic in these pigeons!"

عمّ مُصْطفى ضِحِك: "و أنا اِكْتشفْت إنّ الجيل الجِديد مُمْكِن يِحِلّ مشاكِل قديمة بِطُرُق جِديدة!"

Uncle Moustafa laughed, "And I discovered that the new generation could solve old problems in new ways!"

بُرْج الحمام

في قلْب الدِّلْتا، حيث النّيل رسم على مرّ السِّنين خريطة مِن التِّرع و المصارِف، و حيْث الأرْض السّوْدا بِترْوي عطش الغيطان الخضْرا، بِيُقف بُرْج حمام عمّ مُصْطفى شامِخ، شاهِد على زمن بِيِتْغيّر. مِن بِعيد، شكْله زيّ المدْنة - رُفيّع و طَويل، بِشبابيكه الخشب المنْقوشة، و الحمام الأبْيَض بِيْطير حَواليْه في دَواير مُتناغْمة، كإنُّه بِيِرْسم حُدود ممْلكة في الهَوا محدِّش يِقْدر يِشوفْها غيْر أهْل الفنّ ده.

عمّ مُصْطفى نفْسُه وَرث البُرْج عن أبوه، اللي وَرثُه عن أبوه. تلات أجْيال شافِت الحمام بِيْطير مِن نفْس الشّبابيك، كُلّ جيل ضاف لِلْبُرْج حِكايَة. جِدُّه بناه مِن الطّوب اللّبِن، حطُّه على أساس مِن حجر جيري قديم. أبوه زوِّد عليْه دوْر، و عملُه القِبّة المُميّزة اللي في السّطْح. و عمّ مُصْطفى نفْسُه حافِظ على التّقاليد، رغْم إنّ الزّمن اِتْغيّر و العالم اِتْغيّر معاه.

"الحمام ده مِش طُيور و خلاص." كان دايْماً يِقول. "ده فنّ و صنْعة و تاريخ. كُلّ حمامة فيهُم بِتِحْكي حدّوتة."

حفيدُه طارِق، طالِب في ثانَوي، كان شايِف المَوْضوع بِعيْن مُخْتلِفة. شابّ مُتعلِّم، بِيْحِبّ العُلوم و التِّكْنولوجْيا، و بِيِقْضي وَقْتُه بيْن الكُتُب و الموبايْل. بِالنِّسْبالُه، بُرْج الحمام كان مُجرّد بقية مِن ماضي معادْش لُه مكان في عالم النِّت و السّوْشْيال ميدِيا.

"يا جِدّو، الدُّنْيا اِتْغيّرِت. النّاس بقِت تبعت رسايِل في ثانْيَة للصين! مين مِحْتاج حمام زاجل دِلْوَقْتي؟"

The Pigeon Tower

In the heart of the Delta, where the Nile has drawn over the years a map of canals and waterways, and where the black soil quenches the thirst of green fields, Uncle Moustafa's pigeon tower stands towering, a witness to changing times. From afar, it looks like a minaret – slim and tall, with its carved wooden windows, and white pigeons flying around it in harmonious circles, as if drawing the boundaries of an aerial kingdom visible only to those who know this art.

Uncle Moustafa himself inherited the tower from his father, who inherited it from his father. Three generations watched pigeons fly from these same windows, each generation adding to the tower's story. His grandfather built it from mud bricks, setting it on a foundation of ancient limestone. His father added a floor and built the distinctive dome on the roof. And Uncle Moustafa himself maintained the traditions, even as time changed and the world with it.

"These pigeons aren't just birds," he would always say. "They're art and craft and history. Each pigeon tells a tale."

His grandson Tarek, a secondary school student, saw things differently. An educated young man, loving science and technology, spending his time between books and mobile phone. For him, the pigeon tower was merely a relic from a past that no longer had a place in the world of internet and social media.

"Grandpa, the world has changed. People now send messages to China in a second! Who needs carrier pigeons nowadays?"

عمّ مُصْطفى كان بِيِبْتِسِم بِهُدوء، و كإنُّه عارِف سِرّ الزّمن. "الحمام مِش لِلرّسايِل بسّ يا طارِق. ده لِلرّوْح... لِلْفنّ... لِلْحُرّية. إنْتَ فاكِر الطّيّارة اِخْترِعت مِنيْن؟ مِن مُراقبِةْ الطُّيور! و البوصْلة بِتاعِةْ موبايْلك؟ الطُّيور عِرْفِت الاِتِّجاهات قبْل البشر بِآلاف السِّنين!"

لكِن المُشْكِلة اللي ظهرِت خلِّت الاِتْنيْن يِفكّروا في المَوْضوع مِن زاوْيَة تانْيَة. حمام عمّ مُصْطفى بدأ يِخْتِفي، واحْدة وَرا التّانْيَة. الأوِّل راحِت "سِتّ الحُسْن"، أجْمل حمامة بيْضا في البُرْج. بعْدها بِيوْميْن اِخْتفى "السُّلْطان"، الشّقْلباظ المشْهور بِحركاتُه في الهَوا. و بعْدها "الملِك"، العبْسي الإسْوِد اللي كان فخْر البُرْج.

عمّ مُصْطفى كان مُتأكِّد إنّ ده شُغْل القرين - الكائِن الخفي اللي النّاس في القرْيَة بِيِحْكوا عنُّه مِن زمان. "أبويا شافُه... كان بِيِظْهر في الفجْر، هُوَّ طَويل أوي، و بِياخُد أحْسن الحمام."

طارِق، بِطبيعِةْ جيلُه المُتشكِّك، قرّر يِحِلّ اللُّغْز بِطريقْتُه. رِكِب كاميرا رقمية في البُرْج، و بِرْنامِج تتبُّع على اللّابْتوْب القديم بِتاعُه. قعد أيّام يراقِب و يِسجِّل كُلّ حاجة: أوْقات طَيَران الحمام، اِتّجاهات الرّيح، حتّى درجات الحرارة.

الحلّ جِهْ في فجْر شِتْوي، و الضّباب لِسّه مِغطّي الغيطان. طارِق شاف صقْر حُرّ، مِن النّوْع المصْري النّادِر، بِيْحوم حَوالِيْن البُرْج. الصّقْر كان جميل و قَوي، ريشُه بُنّي مِحْمِرّ بِيِلْمع في أوِّل ضوْء النّهار.

لمّا بحث في المَوْضوع، اِكْتشف حقيقة مُحْزِنة. المدينة الجِديدة اللي بِيِبْنوها على حُدود القرْيَة خدِت أراضي الصُّقور البرّية. المباني العالْيَة و الشّوارِع الواسْعة قضِت على بيئِتْهُم الطّبيعية. الصُّقور، في كِفاحْها لِلْبقاء، بدأِت تِدوّر على مصادِر جِديدة لِلْغِذاء.

Uncle Moustafa would smile quietly, as if knowing time's secret. "Pigeons aren't just for messages, Tarek. They're for the soul... for art... for freedom. Do you know where the airplane was invented from? From watching birds! And your phone's compass? Birds knew directions thousands of years before humans!"

But the problem that emerged made them both think about the matter from a different angle. Uncle Moustafa's pigeons started disappearing, one after another. First went "Beauty Queen," the most beautiful white pigeon in the tower. Two days later "Sultan" vanished, the Shaqlabaz famous for its aerial acrobatics. Then "King," the black Absi that was the tower's pride.

Uncle Moustafa was sure it was the work of the qareen – the invisible being that village people had spoken about for ages. "My father saw it... it would appear at dawn, very tall, taking the best pigeons."

Tarek, with his generation's skeptical nature, decided to solve the mystery his way. He installed a digital camera in the tower and tracking software on his old laptop. He spent days observing and recording everything: pigeons' flight times, wind directions, even temperatures.

The solution came on a winter dawn, while fog still covered the fields. Tarek saw a free falcon, of the rare Egyptian breed, circling around the tower. The falcon was beautiful and strong, its reddish-brown feathers gleaming in the day's first light.

When he researched the matter, he discovered a sad truth. The new city being built on the village's edge had taken the wild falcons' lands. The high buildings and wide streets had destroyed their natural habitat. The falcons, in their struggle for survival, began searching for new food sources.

"شُفْت يا طارِق؟" قال عمّ مُصْطفى لمّا عِرِف الحقيقة. "حتّى القرين بِيِتْغيّر معَ الزّمن. زمان كان روْح خفية... دِلْوَقْتي بقى ضحية لِلْعُمْران!"

طارِق حسّ إنّ المُشْكِلة أعْمق مِن مُجرّد حمام بِيِخْتِفي. دي كانِت قِصّةْ صِراع قديم بيْن التّطوُّر و الطّبيعة. معَ صُحابُه في المدْرسة و بِمُساعدِةْ مُدرِّس العُلوم، بدأ مشْروع لِإنْقاذ الصُّقور. عملوا محْمِيّات صُغيّرة في الجبل القُريِّب، و بدأوا يِوَثّقوا حَياةْ الطُّيور البرّية في المنْطِقة.

و معَ الوَقْت،بقى البُرْج مِش مُجرّد مكان لِترْبيةْ الحمام. بقى مرْكز صُغيّر لِدِراسةْ الطُّيور، بِيْزورُه طلبِةْ المدارِس و الجامْعات. طارِق نفْسُه بقى خبير في سُلوك الطُّيور، بِيِجْمع بيْن حِكْمِةْ جِدُّه القديمة و العِلْم الحديث.

"تِعْرف يا جِدّو؟" طارِق قال في يوْم و هُوَّ قاعِد معَ جِدُّه في البُرْج بِيْراقْبوا غُروب الشّمْس. "يِمْكِن القرين مكانْش عايِز ياخُد الحمام... يِمْكِن كان بِيْحاوِل يِعلِّمْنا درْس."

عمّ مُصْطفى هزّ راسُه بِابْتِسامة: "في الحَياة يا طارِق، مفيش حاجة بِتْروح على طول. كُلّ اللي بِيِخْتِفي، بِيْسيب وَراه حِكْمة."

دِلْوَقْتي، البُرْج بقى أعْلى مِن الأوِّل، و الحمام بِيْطير أحْلى مِن زمان. و الصُّقور بقِت جُزْء مِن المنْظر الطّبيعي لِلْمكان. و في الفجْر، لمّا تِبُصّ لِلسّما، تِشوف الطُّيور كُلّها بِتْطير معَ بعْض، في رقْصة قديمة قدّ الزّمن نفْسُه.

“See, Tarek?” said Uncle Moustafa when he learned the truth. “Even the qareen changes with time. In the past, it was an invisible spirit... now it’s a victim of urbanization!”

Tarek felt the problem was deeper than just disappearing pigeons. It was a story of an ancient struggle between progress and nature. With his school friends and help from their science teacher, he started a project to save the falcons. They created small sanctuaries in the nearby mountain and began documenting the area’s wild bird life.

Over time, the tower became more than just a place for raising pigeons. It became a small center for bird studies, visited by school and university students. Tarek himself became an expert in bird behavior, combining his grandfather’s old wisdom with modern science.

“You know, Grandpa?” said Tarek one day while sitting with his grandfather in the tower watching the sunset. “Maybe the qareen didn’t want to take the pigeons... maybe it was trying to teach us a lesson.”

Uncle Moustafa nodded with a smile, “In life, Tarek, nothing disappears completely. Everything that vanishes leaves wisdom behind.”

Now, the tower stands taller than before, and the pigeons fly more beautifully than ever. And the falcons have become part of the place’s natural scenery. And at dawn, when you look to the sky, you see all the birds flying together, in a dance as old as time itself.

أغاني المدْرسة

The School Songs

Set against the backdrop of the 1919 Egyptian Revolution against British occupation, this story takes place in a rural Delta village. At this time, education in Egypt occurred primarily in كُتّاب *kuttāb* – traditional schools where children learned reading, writing, and Quranic studies. The kuttab system was particularly important in rural areas, where it was often the only form of education available. These schools typically consisted of a single room or courtyard where students of different ages would learn together under one teacher.

Key Vocabulary

- كُتّاب (*kuttāb*) – traditional elementary school for teaching reading, writing, and Quran
- مُدرِّسة (*mudarrísa*) – female teacher
- بيْه (*bē*) – title of respect used in Ottoman Egypt and early 20th century
- تُراث (*turās*) – heritage, traditions
- الثَّوْرة (*issáwra*) – the revolution
- حجْلة (*hágla*) – hopscotch, a traditional children's game
- الغُمّيْضة (*ilɣummēḍa*) – hide and seek
- أعيان البلد (*ʔa3yān ilbálad*) – village notables
- مدْرسةِ المُعلِّمات (*madrásit ilmu3allimāt*) – Teachers' College for women
- مرْكز الشُّرْطة (*márakaz iššúrṭa*) – police station
- الإنْجِليز (*ilʔingilīz*) – the English (British)
- مُظاهْرة (*muẓáhra*) – demonstration
- بَيْرم التّونْسي (*báyram ittúnsi*) – Bayram Al-Tunsi, famous Egyptian poet of the era known for revolutionary verses

The School Songs	ʔaɣāni -lmadrása	أغاني المدْرسة
Long ago in Egypt.	*zamān fi maṣr.*	زمان في مصْر.
Umnia is a teacher.	*ʔumníyya mudarrísa.*	أُمْنية مُدرِّسة.
She loves Egypt.	*bitḥíbbᵊ maṣr.*	بِتْحِبّ مصْر.
At school:	*fi -lmadrása:*	في المدْرسة:
– She teaches children	*– bit3állim ilʔawlād*	- بِتْعلِّم الأَوْلاد
– She sings with them	*– bitɣanni ma3āhum*	- بِتْغنّي معاهُم
– She tells them stories	*– bitiḥkílhum qíṣaṣ*	- بِتِحْكيلْهُم قِصص
The children sing:	*ilʔawlād biyɣánnu:*	الأَوْلاد بِيْغنّوا:
"Our country is beautiful	*baládna ḥílwa*	"بلدْنا حِلْوَة
Our country is precious	*baládna ɣálya*	بلدْنا غالْيَة
We love it"	*ʔíḥna binḥibbáha*	إحْنا بِنْحِبّها"
Mohammed is a student at school.	*mᵊḥámmad tilmīz fī ilmadrása.*	محمّد تِلْميذ في المدْرسة.
His father works with the English.	*ʔabū biyištáɣal má3a -lʔingilīz.*	أبوه بِيِشْتغل معَ الإنْجِليز.

Mohammed sings at home.	*mᵊħámmad biyɣánni fi -lbēt.*	محمّد بِيْغنّي في البيْت.
His father heard the song.	*ʔabū símiʕ ilʔuɣníyya.*	أبوه سِمِع الأُغْنية.
He went to school.	*rāħ ilmadrása.*	راح المدْرسة.
He said, “I love Egypt, too!”	*ʔāl: “ʔána kamān baħíbbᵊ maʂr!”*	قال: "أنا كمان بحِبّ مصْر!"
Now:	*dilwaʔtī:*	دِلْوَقْتي:
– Mohammed’s father helps	*– ʔabū m(ᵊ)ħámmad biysāʕid*	- أبو محمّد بِيْساعِد
– The children learn	*– ilʔawlād biyitʕallímu*	- الأَوْلاد بِيِتْعلِّموا
– Umnia is happy	*– ʔumníyya mabsūʈa*	- أُمْنية مبْسوطة
Everyone sings.	*kull innās bitɣánni.*	كُلّ النّاس بِتْغنّي.
Everyone loves Egypt.	*kull innās bitħíbbᵊ maʂr.*	كُلّ النّاس بِتْحِبّ مصْر.
Egypt became free.	*maʂrᵊ báʔit ħúrra.*	مصْر بقِت حُرّة.

The School Songs	أغاني المدْرسة
1919, in a small Delta village. Umnia is a young teacher in the kuttab. She loves the students and teaches them in a beautiful way.	سنِةْ ١٩١٩ في قرْيَة صُغيّرة في الدِّلْتا. أُمْنية مُدرِّسة شابّة في الكُتّاب. بِتْحِبّ التّلاميذ و بِتْعلِّمْهُم بِطريقة حِلْوَة.
Every day, the students play in the courtyard and sing songs. Umnia chooses special games and songs:	كُلّ يوْم، التّلاميذ بِيِلْعبوا في الحوْش و يِغنّوا أغاني. أُمْنية بِتِخْتار ألْعاب و أغاني خاصّة:
"Oh our precious country	"يا بلدْنا يا غالْيَة
Oh our high land	يا أرْضِنا العالْيَة
We protect you with our souls	نِحْميكي بِأرْواحْنا
From any oppressive hand"	مِن أيّ إيد ظالْمة"
In class, she tells them stories about ancient Egypt and Egyptian heroes.	في الفصْل، بِتِحْكيلْهُم قِصص عن مصْر القديمة و الأبْطال المصْرِيّين.
Mohammed, son of Gamal Bey who works with the English, loves the school songs very much. At home, he sings to the family:	محمّد، إبْن جمال بيْه اللي بِيِشْتغل معَ الإنْجِليز، بِيْحِبّ أغاني المدْرسة أوي. في البيْت، بِيْغنّي لِلْعيْلة:
Oh our precious country...	يا بلدْنا يا غالْيَة...

His father heard the song and understood its meaning. He went to school to meet Umnia.	أبوه سِمِع الأُغْنية و عِرِف معْناها. راح المدْرسة يِقابِل أُمْنية.
Umnia was scared. But Gamal Bey said:	أُمْنية خافِت. بسّ جمال بيْه قال:
"Don't be afraid, Miss. I also love Egypt."	"متْخافيش يا أُسْتاذة. أنا كمان بحِبّ مصْر."
He took a paper from his pocket, "Take this, it's a new song for the children."	طلّع مِن جيْبُه وَرقة: "خُدي، دي أُغْنية جِديدة لِلأَوْلاد."
Umnia read the paper and her eyes filled with tears. It was a new patriotic song.	أُمْنية قرِت الوَرقة و عيْنيْها دمّعِت. كانِت أُغْنية وَطنية جِديدة.
Now, Gamal Bey helps Umnia:	دِلْوَقْتي، جمال بيْه بِيْساعِد أُمْنية:
– He brings her new books	- بِيْجيبْلها كُتُب جِديدة
– He protects the school	- بِيِحْمي المدْرسة
– He encourages families to send their children to the kuttab	- بِيْشجّع الأهالي يِوَدّوا وِلادْهُم الكُتّاب
And every day the students sing, play, and learn:	و التّلاميذ كُلّ يوْم بِيْغنّوا و يِلْعبوا و يِتْعلِّموا:
– Love for Egypt	- حُبّ مصْر

- الشّجاعة	– Courage
- الأمل في بُكْره	– Hope for tomorrow
بعْد سِنين، لمّا مصْر خدِت حُرّيتْها، كان فيه جيل كامِل مِن الأَوْلاد فاهْمين يَعْني أيْه وَطن.	Years later, when Egypt gained its freedom, there was a whole generation of children who understood what homeland means.

أغاني المدْرسة

The School Songs

في سنةْ ١٩١٩، و الثّوْرة مُولّعة في كُلّ حِتّة في مصر، كانِت أُمْنية بِتمْشي كُلّ يوْم مِن بيْتْهُم لِحدّ الكُتّاب على حُدود القرْيَة. شابّة في العِشْرينات، مِتْعلِّمة في مدْرِسةْ المُعلِّمات، و مُؤْمِنة إنّ التّعْليم هُوَّ أوِّل خطْوَة لِلْحُرّية.

In 1919, with revolution burning in every part of Egypt, Umnia walked every day from her house to the kuttab at the village's edge. A young woman in her twenties, educated at the Teachers' College, and believing that education was the first step to freedom.

في الكُتّاب، أُمْنية مِش بِتْعلِّم القِرايَة و الكِتابة بسّ. كُلّ يوْم في الفُسْحة، بِتْجمّع الأَوْلاد في الحوْش و تِعلِّمْهُم ألْعاب و أغاني مِن التُّراث المصْري القديم. بسّ الألْعاب دي كان ليها معْنى خاصّ:

In the kuttab, Umnia didn't just teach reading and writing. Every day during break time, she would gather the children in the courtyard and teach them games and songs from old Egyptian heritage. But these games had special meaning:

لمّا يِلْعبوا حجْلة، تِرْسِم على الأرْض خريطِةْ مصر، و الأَوْلاد يِنْطّوا مِن مُحافْظة لمُحافْظة و هُمّا بِيْغنّوا:

When they played Hopscotch, she would draw Egypt's map on the ground, and the children would jump from province to province while singing:

يا بلدْنا يا غالْيَة
يا أرْضِنا العالْيَة
نِحْميكي بِأرْواحْنا
مِن أيّ إيد ظالْمة

Oh our precious country
Oh our high land
We protect you with our souls
From any oppressive hand

و لمّا يِلْعبوا "العسْكر و الحرامية"، تِخلّي الأَوْلاد الوَطنِيّين هُمّا الأبْطال:

And when they played "Soldiers and Thieves," she would make the nationalist children the heroes:

إحْنا جُنود الوَطن
نِحْمي البلد و السّكن

We are the soldiers of our homeland
We protect the country and dwellings

محمّد، إبْن جمال بيْه اللي بِيِشْتغل مُترْجِم معَ الإنْجِليز في المرْكز، كان مِن أذْكى التّلاميذ. حفظ كُلّ الأغاني و فِهِم معانيها. في البيْت، قعد يِغنّي لإخْواتُه الصُّغيّرين، و أبوه سِمْعُه.

Mohammed, son of Gamal Bey (who worked as a translator with the English at the district office), was one of the brightest students. He memorized all the songs and understood their meanings. At home, he sat singing to his younger siblings, and his father heard him.

جمال بيْه، اللي كان معْروف إنُّه قُريِّب مِن الإنْجليز، راح الكُتّاب يقابل أُمْنية. قلْبها وِقِف مِن الخوْف، فاكْرة إنُّه جايّ يِبلّغ عنْها.

Gamal Bey, who was known to be close to the English, went to the kuttab to meet Umnia. Her heart stopped in fear, thinking he was coming to report her.

"متْخافيش يا أُسْتاذة." قال بِصوْت هادي. "الإنْجليز فاكْرين إنُّهُم بِيِسْتخْدِموني، بسّ أنا في الحقيقة بساعِد الثُّوّار. و أنا جايّ أشْكُرك - إنْتي بِتِزْرعي الوَطنية في قُلوب جيل جِديد."

"Don't be afraid, Miss," he said in a quiet voice. "The English think they're using me, but I'm actually helping the revolutionaries. And I've come to thank you – you're planting patriotism in the hearts of a new generation."

طلّع مِن جيْبُه وَرقة: "دي أُغْنية جِديدة كتبْها الشّاعِر بيْرم التّونْسي. مُمْكِن تِعلّميها لِلأوْلاد؟"

He took a paper from his pocket. "This is a new song written by poet Bayram Al-Tunsi. Can you teach it to the children?"

أُمْنية قرِت الأُغْنية و عيْنيْها دمّعِت. مِن اليوْم ده، بقى جمال بيْه حليف سِرّي ليها:

Umnia read the song and her eyes filled with tears. From that day, Gamal Bey became her secret ally:

- بيْجيبْلها كُتُب وَطنية
- بيْحذّرْها لمّا يِكون فيه تفْتيش
- بيِقْنِع الأهالي يِسيبوا بناتْهُم يِتْعلّموا

– He brought her nationalist books
– He warned her when inspections were coming
– He convinced families to let their daughters learn

الكُتّاب بقى مرْكز صُغيّر لِلْوَطنية. الأَوْلاد بِيِتْعلِّموا القِرايَة و الكِتابه، و في نفْس الوَقْت بِيِفْهموا معْنى الحُرّية مِن خِلال الأغاني و الألْعاب.

The kuttab became a small center for patriotism. The children learned reading and writing, while at the same time understanding the meaning of freedom through songs and games.

في يوْم، سِمْعوا صوْت مُظاهْرة في الشّارِع. أُمْنية وِقْفِت قُدّام الشِّبّاك، و الدُّموع في عيْنيْها، و قالِت: "شايْفين يا وِلاد؟ دي مصْر بِتْنادي عليْنا."

One day, they heard the sound of a demonstration in the street. Umnia stood at the window, tears in her eyes, and said, "See, children? That's Egypt calling us."

محمّد رفع إيدُه و قال: "وإحْنا سِمِعْنا النِّداء يا أُسْتاذة!"

Mohammed raised his hand and said, "And we've heard the call, Miss!"

بعْد سِنين طَويلة، لمّا مصْر اِسْتقلِّت، كان الجيل اللي اِتْربّى في كُتّاب أُمْنية مِن أحْسن المُدافِعين عن حُقوق مصْر. كُلّ ما حدّ يِسْألْهُم إزّاي اِتْعلِّموا حُبّ الوَطن، يِقولوا: "مِن أغاني المدْرسة!"

Many years later, when Egypt gained independence, the generation that grew up in Umnia's kuttab became among the best defenders of Egypt's rights. Whenever anyone asked them how they learned to love their homeland, they would say, "From the school songs!"

أغاني المدْرسة

في فِبْرايِر ١٩١٩، و التَّوْرة بِتِشْتعل في شَوارِع القاهِرة، كانِت أُمْنية قاعْدة في أوْضة صُغيّرة في بيْتْهُم في الدِّلْتا، بِتِكْتِب في دفْتر خبِّت فيه أسْرارْها و أحْلامْها. خريجِةْ مدْرسِةْ المُعلِّمات، و بِنْت واحِد مِن أعْيان البلد اللي رفض يِشْتغل معَ الإنْجِليز و فِضِل يِزْرع أرْضُه بِنفْسُه.

كتبِت في دفْترْها: لَوْ مقْدِرْناش نِحْمِل السِّلاح، نِقْدر نِربّي جيل يِعْرف يَعْني أيْه وَطن.

في الكُتّاب اللي في حُدود القرْيَة، كانِت أُمْنية بِتِنْسِج ثَوْرِتْها الخاصّة، خيْط خيْط، في عُقول و قُلوب تلاميذْها. مِن أيّام جِدِّتْها و البنات في القرْيَة مبِيْروحوش المدارِس، بسّ هِيَّ صمِّمِت تِغيّر العادة دي.

كُلّ صباح، و قبْل ما تِبْدأ دُروس القِرايَة و الكِتابة، كانِت تِجمّع الأَوْلاد في دايْرة و تِعلِّمْهُم الألْعاب القديمة. الحجْلة بقِت خريطِةْ مصْر، و الغُمّيْضة بقِت لِعْبة عن الثُّوّار و المُحْتلّين، و كُلّ أُغْنية شعْبية بقى ليها معْنى جِديد:

"طِلْعِت يا محْلا نورْها طِلْعِت

شمْس الحُرّية طِلْعِت

وإن كان حدّ يِسْأل علِيْنا

إحْنا وِلاد مصْر طِلِعْنا"

The School Songs

In February 1919, as revolution blazed through Cairo's streets, Umnia sat in a small room in her Delta home, writing in a notebook where she kept her secrets and dreams. A Teachers' College graduate, daughter of a village notable who refused to work with the English and chose to farm his land himself.

She wrote in her notebook, "If we cannot carry weapons, we can raise a generation that knows what homeland means."

In the kuttab at the village's edge, Umnia was weaving her own revolution, thread by thread, in her students' minds and hearts. Since her grandmother's time, village girls didn't go to school, but she was determined to change this custom.

Every morning, before reading and writing lessons began, she would gather the children in a circle and teach them old games. Hopscotch became Egypt's map, hide-and-seek became a game about revolutionaries and occupiers, and every folk song gained new meaning:

"It rose, how beautiful its light rose

The sun of freedom rose

And if anyone asks about us

We are Egypt's children, we have risen"

محمّد، إبْن جمال بيْه المُترْجِم في مرْكز الشُّرْطة، كان مِن أذْكى التّلاميذ و أكْترْهُم فهْماً لِلرّسايِل المِسْتخْبية في الأغاني و الألْعاب. في البيْت، قعد يِغنّي لِإخْواتُه و أُمُّه تِسقّف معاه:

"يا مصْر يا أُمّ البِلاد

يا أرْض خضْرا بِتْجودي

هنِحْميكي بِالرّوْح و الدّمّ"

ونْخلّيكي تاني تِعودي" جمال بيْه سِمِع صوْت إبْنُه في الصّالوْن. وِقِف يِسْمع مِن وَرا الباب، و قلْبُه بِيُرْقُص معَ الكِلمات. و الصُّبْح، راح الكُتّاب.

أُمْنية شافِتُه داخِل، و حسِّت إنّ قلْبها وِقِف. عُمْرها ما نِسْيِت اليوْم ده: أبوها في السِّجْن بِتُهْمِةْ التّحْريض ضِدّ الإنْجِليز، و أخوها مُخْتفي في القاهِرة بعْد مُظاهرات الطّلبة. دِلْوَقْتي، جمال بيْه، اللي معْروف إنُّه عيْن الإنْجِليز في البلد، واقِف قُدّامْها.

"الأغاني دي خطر يا أُسْتاذة." قال بِصوْت واطي: "بس أحْلى خطر سِمِعْتُه في حَياتي."

طلّع مِن جيْبْتُه وَرقة مِطبّقة: "دي قصيدة جِديدة لِبَيْرم التّونْسي. لِسّه طابْعينْها في السِّرّ. مُمْكِن تِضيفيها لِلْمنْهج بِتاعِك؟"

مِن اليوْم ده، بقى الكُتّاب خلية نحْل سِرّية. جمال بيْه يِجيب الكُتُب و المنْشورات مِخبّيها في عربيةْ الخُضار، و أُمْنية تِحوّل الكِلمات لِألْعاب و أغاني. الأوْلاد يِتْعلِّموا و يِفْهموا، و يِرْجعوا البيْت يِزْرعوا البُذور في عيْلِتْهُم.

Mohammed, son of Gamal Bey the translator at the police station, was among the brightest students and most understanding of the messages hidden in songs and games. At home, he would sing to his siblings while his mother clapped along:

"Oh Egypt, mother of all lands

Oh green land, you give generously

We'll protect you with soul and blood

And make you return again"

Gamal Bey heard his son's voice in the sitting room. He stood listening behind the door, his heart dancing with the words. In the morning, he went to the kuttab.

Umnia saw him enter and felt her heart stop. She never forgot that day: her father in prison for inciting against the English, her brother disappeared in Cairo after student demonstrations. Now, Gamal Bey, known as the English's eyes in the village, stood before her.

"These songs are dangerous, Miss," he said in a low voice. "But the most beautiful danger I've ever heard."

He pulled out a folded paper from his pocket, "This is a new poem by Bayram Al-Tunsi. They just printed it secretly. Could you add it to your special curriculum?"

From that day, the kuttab became a secret beehive. Gamal Bey would bring books and pamphlets hidden in vegetable carts, and Umnia would transform the words into games and songs. The children would learn and understand, returning home to plant seeds in their families.

في ليْلة مِن لَيالي رمضان، و القرْيَة كُلّها صاحْيَة، دخل البوليس الإنْجِليزي يِفتِّش البِيوت. في بيْت أُمْنية، دوّروا في كُلّ حِتّة. لكِن محدِّش فكّر يِفتِّش كُرّاسات التّلاميذ، وَلا يِسْأل عن معْنى الألْعاب في الحوْش.

بعْد سِنين طَويلة، لمّا خرج الإنْجِليز مِن مصْر، كان فيه جيل كامِل مِن أَوْلاد القرْيَة فاهْمين يَعْني أيْه وَطن. و لمّا حدّ يِسْألْهُم مين علِّمْهُم الوَطنية، يِقولوا: "مُدرِّسة في كُتّاب صُغيّر، حوِّلت الخوْف لِأغاني، و الألْعاب لِثَوْرة، و الأطْفال لِأبْطال."

في آخِر أيّامْها، و أُمْنية قاعْدة في نفْس الأوْضة اللي كانِت بِتِكْتِب فيها مِن سِتّين سنة، فتحِت الدّفْتر القديم و كتبِت: "الثّوْرة مِش دايْماً بِتِبْقى في الشّوارِع... ساعات بِتِبْقى في أُغْنية بسيطة، في لِعْبة عِيال، في حِلْم بُكْره."

One Ramadan night, with the whole village awake, English police entered to search houses. In Umnia's house, they searched everywhere. But no one thought to check students' notebooks, or ask about the meaning of games in the courtyard.

Years later, when the English left Egypt, there was an entire generation of village children who understood what homeland meant. When asked who taught them patriotism, they would say, "A teacher in a small kuttab, who turned fear into songs, games into revolution, and children into heroes."

In her final days, Umnia sitting in the same room where she wrote sixty years ago, opened the old notebook and wrote, "Revolution isn't always in the streets... Sometimes it's in a simple song, in children's games, in tomorrow's dream."

سِرّ الكُشري

The Secret of the Koshari

This story takes place in وِسْط البلد *wisṭ ilbálad* (downtown) in Cairo, specifically on شارِع طلْعت حرْب *šāri3 ṭál3at ḫarb* (Talaat Harb Street), one of its most famous thoroughfares. The tale centers around كُشري *kúshari* (koshari), Egypt's beloved national street food dish made of rice, pasta, lentils, chickpeas, and spicy tomato sauce. In Egyptian urban culture, street food establishments often become neighborhood institutions, with recipes passed down through generations and fierce loyalties developing among customers.

Key Vocabulary

- كُشري (*kúšari*) – popular Egyptian street food combining rice, pasta, lentils, chickpeas, and spicy tomato sauce
- صلْصة (*ṣálṣa*) – sauce
- حاجّ (*ђagg*) – respectful title for an older woman; originally meant someone who completed the pilgrimage to Mecca but now used more broadly
- حاجّة (*ђágga*) – respectful title for an older woman
- بِتاع ــ (*bitā3* __) – vendor/seller of ___
- شطّة (*šáṭṭa*) – hot chili pepper
- طعْمية (*ṭa3míyya*) – Egyptian falafel
- فول (*fūl*) – cooked fava beans
- قطايِف (*ʔaṭāyif*) – sweet dumplings typically served during Ramadan
- محلّ (*maђáll*) – shop; casual restaurant
- زبايِن (*zabāyin*) – customers
- تتْبيلة (*tatbīla*) – seasoning

The Secret of the Koshari	*sirr ilkúšari*	سِرّ الكُشري
In a street downtown:	*fi šāri3 fi wisṭ ilbálad:*	في شارِع في وِسْط البلد:
A koshari shop for Hassan	*maḫállᵊ kúšari li-ḫásan*	محلّ كُشري لِحسن
A koshari shop for Hussein	*maḫállᵊ kúšari li-ḫ(i)sēn*	محلّ كُشري لِحِسيْن
Hassan and Hussein are brothers.	*ḫásan wi ḫ(i)sēn ʔixwāt.*	حسن و حِسيْن إخْوات.
Their father had a koshari shop.	*ʔabūhum kān 3andu maḫállᵊ kúšari.*	أبوهُم كان عنْدُه محلّ كُشري.
Their father died.	*ʔabūhum māt.*	أبوهُم مات.
Each one opened a shop:	*kullᵊ wāḫid fátaḫ maḫáll:*	كُلّ واحِد فتح محلّ:
– Hassan has good sauce	*– ḫásan 3andu ṣálṣa ḫílwa*	- حسن عنْدُه صلْصة حِلْوَة
– Hussein has good rice	*– ḫisēn 3andu rúzzᵊ ḫilw*	- حِسيْن عنْدُه رُزّ حِلْو
The brothers don't talk to each other.	*ilʔixwāt miš biykallímu ba3ḍ.*	الإخْوات مِش بِيْكلِّموا بعْض.

The customers are confused:	*izzabāyin miɧtarīn:*	الزّبايِن مِحْتارين:
– Some people like Hussein's shop	*– nās bitɧíbbᵊ maɧállᵊ ɧ(i)sēn*	- ناس بِتْحِبّ محلّ حِسيْن
– Some people like Hassan's shop	*– nās bitɧíbbᵊ maɧállᵊ ɧásan*	- ناس بِتْحِبّ محلّ حسن
Their mother visited the shops:	*ʔummúhum zārit ilmaɧallēn:*	أُمُّهُم زارِت المحلّيْن:
"Hassan, is the sauce like I taught you?"	*"ɧásan, iʂʂálʂa zayyᵊ ma 3allímtak?"*	"حسن، الصّلْصة زيّ ما علِّمْتك؟"
"Hussein, is the rice like I taught you?"	*"ɧisēn, irrúzzᵊ zayyᵊ ma 3allímtak?"*	"حِسيْن، الرُّزّ زيّ ما علِّمْتك؟"
The brothers are surprised:	*ilʔixwāt mistaɣrabīn:*	الإخْوات مِسْتغْربين:
"You taught us the koshari, Mom?"	*"ʔínti 3allimtīna -lkúšari ya māma?"*	"إنْتي علِّمْتينا الكُشري يا ماما؟"
Mom laughed:	*māma ɖíɧkit:*	ماما ضِحْكِت:
"Yes, each of you is good at something!"	*"ʔáywa, kullᵊ wāɧid fīkum ɧilwᵊ f(i) ɧāga!"*	"أَيْوَه، كُلّ واحِد فيكُم حِلْو في حاجة!"
Now:	*dilwáʔti:*	دِلْوَقْتي:
– The brothers love each other	*– ilʔixwāt biyɧíbbu ba3ɖ*	- الإخْوات بِيْحِبّوا بعْض

– The shop is one big shop	*– ilmaḫállᵊ wāḫid kibīr*	- المحلّ واحِد كِبير
– All people are happy	*– innās kulláha mabsūṭa*	- النّاس كُلّها مبْسوطة
– Mom is happy	*– māma farḫāna*	- ماما فرْحانة

A2

The Secret of the Koshari	سِرّ الكُشري
On a famous street in downtown, there are two koshari shops facing each other:	في شارِع مشْهور في وِسْط البلد، فيه محلّيْن كُشري مِتْقابْلين:
Hajj Mahmoud's Original Koshari	كُشري الحاجّ محْمود الأصْلي
and Hajj Mahmoud's Real Koshari	و كُشري الحاجّ محْمود الحقيقي
The shops belong to Hassan and Hussein, Hajj Mahmoud's sons. The brothers haven't spoken to each other for a year, since their father died.	المحلّيْن بِتوع حسن و حِسيْن، وِلاد الحاجّ محْمود. الأخّيْن مِش بِيْكلِّموا بعْض مِن سنة، مِن يوْم ما أبوهُم تَوَفّى.
Hassan said, "I have Dad's original recipe!"	حسن قال: "أنا عنْدي الوَصْفة الأصْلية بِتاعِةْ بابا!"
Hussein replied, "No, I have the real recipe!"	حِسيْن ردّ: "لأ، أنا عنْدي الوَصْفة الحقيقية!"
Each one opened a shop. Each one made a big sign. And the customers don't know where to go!	كُلّ واحِد فتح محلّ. كُلّ واحِد عامِل لافْتة كِبيرة. و الزّبايِن مِش عارْفين يِروحوا فيْن!
"Hassan's sauce is better!"	"الصّلْصة بِتاعِةْ حسن أحْلى!"
"No, Hussein's sauce is more delicious!"	"لأ، الصّلْصة بِتاعِةْ حِسيْن أطْعم!"

One day, Hagga Neamat, their mother, visited both shops. First, she went to Hassan.	في يوْم، الحاجة نِعْمات، أُمُّهُم، زارِت المحلّيْن. الأوِّل راحِت لِحسن.
"How are you, my dear? Are you making the koshari like I taught you?"	"إزّيّك يا حبيبي؟ عامِل الكُشري زيّ ما علِّمْتك؟"
Then she went to Hussein.	و بعْديْن راحِت لِحسيْن.
"How are you, my soul? Is the koshari exactly as I told you?"	"إزّيّك يا روْحي؟ عملْت الكُشري زيّ ما قُلْتِلك بِالظّبْط؟"
The brothers were surprised. "You taught us how to make koshari?"	الأخّيْن اِسْتغْربوا. "إنْتي علِّمْتينا إزّاي نِعْمِل الكُشري؟"
Hagga Neamat laughed. "Yes, boys. Your father, may God rest his soul, had one recipe. But I taught each of you a slightly different way."	الحاجة نِعْمات ضِحْكِت: "أيْوَه يا وِلاد. أبوكُم الله يِرْحمُه كان عنْدُه وَصْفة واحْدة. بسّ أنا علِّمْت كُلّ واحِد فيكُم بِطريقة مُخْتلِفة شُوَيّة."
"Why, Mom?"	"ليْه يا ماما؟"
"So each of you would have your own special koshari. No need for problems. People love both!"	"عشان كُلّ واحِد يِعْمِل كُشري خاصّ بيه. مفيش داعي لِلْمشاكِل. النّاس بِتْحِبّ الاِتْنيْن!"
Hassan and Hussein looked at each other. Finally, they understood.	حسن و حِسيْن بصّوا لِبعْض. أخيراً فِهْموا.

Now:	دِلْوَقْتي:
– The shops are next to each other	- المحلّيْن جنْب بعْض
– The brothers are talking again	- الأخّيْن رِجْعوا يِكلِّموا بعْض تاني
– Customers eat here one day and there another	- الزّبايِن بِياكْلوا يوْم هِنا و يوْم هِناك
– And Hagga Neamat is happy her sons are back together	- و الحاجة نِعْمات مبْسوطة إنّ وِلادْها رِجْعوا لِبعْض
“You know what?” she told them one day, “The best flavor in koshari... is the taste of love!”	“تِعْرفوا؟” قالِتْلُهُم يوْم. “أحْلى طعْم في الكُشري... طعْم المحبّة!”

B1

سِرّ الكُشري

The Secret of the Koshari

في شارِع طلْعت حرْب، مِن أشْهر شَوارِع وِسْط البلد، كان فيه حاجة غريبة بِتِلْفِت نظر كُلّ اللي بِيْعدّي: محلّيْن كُشري قُصاد بعْض، يُفطْهُم حمْرا و صفْرا كِبيرة، و كُلّ محلّ مكْتوب عليْه إنُّه الأصْلي.

On Talaat Harb Street, one of downtown's most famous streets, there was a strange phenomenon that caught every passerby's attention: two koshari shops facing each other, with large red and yellow signs, each claiming to be the original.

كُشري الحاجّ محْمود الأصْلي - مُنْذُ ١٩٨٥
و كُشري الحاجّ محْمود الحقيقي - الفرْع الرّئيسي

Hajj Mahmoud's Original Koshari – Since 1985
and Hajj Mahmoud's Real Koshari – Main Branch

المحلّيْن دوْل بِتوع حسن و حِسيْن، وِلاد الحاجّ محْمود اللي كان أشْهر واحِد بِيعْمِل كُشري في المنْطِقة. بعْد ما الحاجّ محْمود تَوَفّى السّنة اللي فاتِت، الأخّيْن اِتْخانْقوا على وَصْفِةْ الكُشري بِتاعْتُه. كُلّ واحِد فيهُم فتح محلّ، و كُلّ واحِد مُقْتنع إنّ عنْدُه النّسْخة الأصْلية مِن الوَصْفة السِّرّية.

These shops belonged to Hassan and Hussein, sons of Hajj Mahmoud who was the most famous koshari maker in the area. After Hajj Mahmoud passed away last year, the brothers fought over his koshari recipe. Each opened his own shop, convinced he had the original version of the secret recipe.

حسن، الأخّ الكِبير، بِيِفْتِخِر بِالصّلْصة الحمْرا بِتاعْتُه: "دي الصّلْصة اللي كان بابا بِيِعْمِلْها بِإيدُه. حرّاقة و مِتبِّلة على أُصولْها."

Hassan, the older brother, took pride in his red sauce. "This is the sauce that Dad used to make with his own hands. Spicy and perfectly seasoned."

حِسيْن، الأخّ الصُّغيّر، مشْهور بِدِقِّةْ مقادير الرُّزّ و المكرونة و العدْس: "بابا علِّمْني إزّاي أسْلُق كُلّ حاجة بِالظّبْط. مفيش حبِّةْ رُزّ بِتِلْزق في التّانْيَة."

Hussein, the younger brother, was famous for his precise measurements of rice, pasta, and lentils. "Dad taught me exactly how to boil everything. Not a single grain of rice sticks to another."

الزّبايِن اِنْقسموا لِفريقيْن. ناس بِتْحِبّ كُشري حسن عشان الصّلْصة الحرّاقة، و ناس بِتْحِبّ كُشري حِسيْن عشان الرُّزّ المظْبوط. حتّى دكاكين الشّارِع اِنْقسمِت: بِتاع الفول وِقِف معَ حسن، و بِتاع العصير وِقِف معَ حِسيْن.

The customers divided into two camps. Some loved Hassan's koshari for the spicy sauce, and others loved Hussein's for the perfect rice. Even the street shops took sides: the foul seller stood with Hassan, and the juice seller stood with Hussein.

في نُصّ الصّيْف، و الحرّ شِديد، و الزّبايِن واقْفين في طابوريْن قُدّام المحلّيْن، الحاجّة نِعْمات قرّرِت تِتْدخّل. زارِت المحلّيْن في نفْس اليوْم.

In mid-summer, with the intense heat, and customers standing in two lines in front of the shops, Hagga Neamat decided to intervene. She visited both shops on the same day.

دخلِت الأوِّل عنْد حسن: "إزّيّك يا حبيب قلْب ماما؟ الصّلْصة عامِلْها زيّ ما قُلْتِلك؟ فاكِر؟ تلات معالِق شطّة، و بصْلة مِحمّرة كُوَيِّس..."

First, she entered Hassan's. "How are you, Mom's sweetheart? Making the sauce like I told you? Remember? Three spoons of chili, and onions well-browned..."

و بعْديْن راحِت لِحسيْن: "إزّيّك يا نور عيْني؟ الرُّزّ مظْبوط زيّ ما علِّمْتك؟ فاكِر؟ شُوَيّةْ زيْت في المايّة المغْلية، و الملْح بعْد ما المايّة تِغْلي..."

Then she went to Hussein's. "How are you, light of my eyes? The rice perfect like I taught you? Remember? A little oil in the boiling water, and salt after the water boils..."

الأخّيْن اِسْتغْربوا. كُلّ واحِد طِلِع مِن محلُّه وِقِف في نُصّ الشّارِع.

The brothers were surprised. Each one came out of his shop and stood in the middle of the street.

"يا ماما، إنْتي اللي علِّمْتينا الوَصْفات دي؟"

"Mom, you taught us these recipes?"

"إحْنا كُنّا فاكْرين إنّها وَصْفِةْ بابا!"

"We thought they were Dad's recipe!"

الحاجّة نِعْمات ضِحْكِت و قالِت: "تعالوا يا وِلاد، اُقْعُدوا معايا في الكافيْه ده."

Hagga Neamat laughed and said, "Come, boys, sit with me in this coffee shop."

في الكافيْه، شرحِتْلُهُم : "أبوكُم ، اللّه يِرْحمُه، كان عنْدُه وَصْفة واحْدة. بسّ أنا شُفْت إنّ كُلّ واحِد فيكُم عنْدُه مَوْهِبة مُخْتلِفة. إنْتَ يا حسن إيدك حِلْوَة في التّتْبيلة و الصّلْصة، و إنْتَ يا حِسيْن مقاديرك مظْبوطة . فا قرّرْت أطوّر مَوْهِبِةْ كُلّ واحِد فيكُم. علِّمْت حسن سِرّ الصّلْصة، و علِّمْت حِسيْن سِرّ الرُّزّ و العدْس."

In the café, she explained, "Your father, may God rest his soul, had one recipe. But I saw that each of you had a different talent. You, Hassan, have a good hand with seasoning and sauce, and you, Hussein, are precise with measurements. So I decided to develop each of your talents. I taught Hassan the secret of the sauce, and taught Hussein the secret of rice and lentils."

"ليْه يا ماما؟" الاِتْنيْن سألوا في نفْس الوَقْت.

"Why, Mom? they both asked at the same time."

"عشان كُلّ واحِد يِكون مُميّز. مِش لازِم تِبْقوا نُسْخِةْ مِن بعْض. و كمان... النّاس بِتْحِبّ التّنوُّع. في زبايِن بِتاكُل هِنا النّهارْده و هِناك بُكْره!"

"So each of you would be special. You don't need to be copies of each other. Also... people like variety. There are customers who eat here today and there tomorrow!"

حسن و حِسيْن بصّوا لِبعْض و اِبْتسموا. كُلّ المشاكِل اللي فاتِت باظِت في لحْظة.

Hassan and Hussein looked at each other and smiled. All the past problems dissolved in a moment.

دِلْوَقْتي، المحلّيْن بقوا جنْب بعْض في نفْس الجِهة مِن الشّارِع. الطّابور بقى واحِد، و الزّباين بيجرّبوا الاِتْنيْن. حسن بِيِعْمِل أحْلى صلْصة في المنْطِقة، و حِسيْن بِيِعْمِل أحْسن رُزّ و عدْس. و الحاجّة نِعْمات بِتيجي كُلّ يوْم جُمْعة تاكُل عنْد واحِد فيهُم بِالدّوْر.

Now, the shops are next to each other on the same side of the street. The line has become one, and customers try both. Hassan makes the best sauce in the area, and Hussein makes the best rice and lentils. And Hagga Neamat comes every Friday to eat at one of their shops in turns.

في الشّارِع دِلْوَقْتي يَفْطة جِديدة:
كُشري الحاجّ محْمود - الأخّيْن حسن و حِسيْن

On the street now, there's a new sign:
Hajj Mahmoud's Koshari – The Brothers Hassan and Hussein

و تحْتها مكْتوب بِخطّ صُغيّر:
الطّعْم اللي معْمول بحُبّ

And written below in small print:
The taste made by love

سِرّ الكُشري

في شارِع طلْعت حرب، يَعْني التّاريخ محْفور في كُلّ رُكْن، يَعْني ريحِةْ الطّعْمية و الفول معَ ريحِةْ الكُتُب القديمة و ضجيج المُرور، كانِت المُنافْسة بيْن محلّيْن كُشري قُصاد بعْض تِمثِّل حِكايَة مصْرية خالِصة. مِش مُجرّد حِكايِةْ طبق شعْبي، ده صِراع عائِلي ملْحمي على تُراث الحاجّ محْمود، ملِك الكُشري في المنْطِقة.

اليُفط الكِبيرة كانِت بِتْشِدّ اللي رايِح و اللي جايّ:

كُشري الحاجّ محْمود الأصْلي - بِنفْس الطّعْم مُنْذُ ١٩٨٥

و كُشري الحاجّ محْمود الحقيقي - طريقِةْ العيْلة الأصْلية

حسن و حِسيْن، الأخّيْن اللي وَرثوا مِهْنِةْ أبوهُم، كانوا زيّ كُلّ الإخْوات المصْرِيّين - مُخْتلِفين في كُلّ حاجة إلّا حُبُّهم لِبعْض، حتّى لَوْ الحُبّ ده مِسْتخبّي تحْت طبقات مِن العِنْد و الكِبْرِياء. حسن، الإبْن الكِبير اللي فِضِل جنْب أبوه في المحلّ مِن صُغْره، كان مُقْتِنِع إنّ صلْصِةْ الكُشري هِيَّ روْح الطّبق. و حِسيْن، اللي درس في معْهد السِّياحة و الفنادِق، كان بِيْجادِل إنّ سِرّ الكُشري في تناسُق المُكوِّنات و طريقِةْ السّلْق.

"الكُشري اللي ملوش صلْصة حرّاقة زيّ النُكْتة اللي ملْهاش قفْلة!" كان حسن بِيْقول لِزبايْنُه و هُوَّ بِيْضيف شُوَيِّةْ شطّة على طلباتْهُم.

"الكُشري فنّ مُتكامِل، مِش مُجرّد صلْصة حمْرا!" كان حِسيْن بِيْرُدّ و هُوَّ بِيْرُصّ الرُّزّ و المكروْنة و العدْس في طبقات مُتناسْقة، كُلّ حبّة في مكانْها.

The Secret of the Koshari

On Talaat Harb Street, where history is carved into every corner, where the smell of falafel and foul mingles with the scent of old books and the the bustle of traffic, the competition between two facing koshari shops represented a purely Egyptian tale. Not just a story about a popular dish, but an epic family struggle over the legacy of Hajj Mahmoud, the area's king of koshari.

The large signs shouted at passersby:

Hajj Mahmoud's Original Koshari – Same Taste Since 1985

and Hajj Mahmoud's Real Koshari – The Original Family Method

Hassan and Hussein, the brothers who inherited their father's profession, were like all Egyptian brothers – different in everything except their love for each other, even if that love was hidden under layers of stubbornness and pride. Hassan, the firstborn who stayed by his father's side in the shop since childhood, believed that koshari sauce was the soul of the dish. And Hussein, who studied at the Tourism and Hotels Institute, argued that koshari's secret lay in the harmony of ingredients and cooking method.

"Koshari without spicy sauce is like a joke without a punchline!" Hassan would tell his customers while adding an extra layer of chili to their orders.

"Koshari is an integrated art, not just red sauce!" Hussein would respond while arranging rice, pasta, and lentils in harmonious layers, each grain in its place.

Amid this competition, the street was divided. The foul seller said Hassan's sauce reminded him of the old days, and the qatayef seller swore that Hussein's method of cooking lentils was the right way. Even the shoe-shiners in front of the shops chose their positions: one in front of Hassan's shop, the other in front of Hussein's.

وِسْط التّنافُس ده، الشّارِع اِتْقسم نُصّيْن. بِتاع الفول بِيْقول إنّ صلْصِةْ حسن بِتْفكّرُه بِأيّام زمان، و صاحِب محلّ القطايِف بِيِحْلِف إنّ طريقِةْ حِسيْن في سلْق العدْس هِيَّ الطّريقة الصّحّ. حتّى اللي بِيِمْسحوا الجِزم قُدّام المحلّيْن اِخْتاروا أماكِنْهُم: واحِد قُدّام محلّ حسن، و التّاني قُدّام محلّ حِسيْن.

الحاجّة نِعْمات، السِّتّ المصْرية الأصيلة اللي ربِّت جيل كامِل في الشّارِع، كانِت بِتْراقِب المشْهد بِحِكْمِةْ الأُمّهات. في يوْم مِن أيّام الصّيْف القاهِري اللي الأسْفلْت فيه بِيْسيح، قرّرِت تِصلّح اللي بيْنْهُم.

دخلِت محلّ حسن و هُوَّ بِيْوَلّع النّار تحْت قِدْرِةْ الصّلْصة: "فاكِر يا حبيبي لمّا كُنْت بعْلِمك سِرّ البصْل المِحمّر؟ قُلْتِلك لازِم تِحمّرُه على نار هادْيَة. الصّبْر هُوَّ المُفْتاح لِلطّعْم الحِلْو."

و بعْديْن راحِت لِحِسيْن و هُوَّ بِيِوْزِن العدْس في ميزان رقمي: "فاكِر يا روْح قلْبي لمّا قُلْتِلك سِرّ نقْع العدْس؟ سِتّ ساعات بِالظّبْط، لا أقلّ وَلا أكْتر."

الأخّيْن وَقّفوا في مكانْهُم. حسن ساب المغْرفة في القِدْرة، و حِسيْن وِقِف يِبُصّ لِأُمُّه بِذُهول.

"مِسْتغْربين؟" اِبْتسمِت الحاجّة نِعْمات. "تعالوا نُقْعُد على قهْوِةْ سِليْمان باشا القديمة، و أحْكيلْكُم الحِكايَة مِن الأوِّل."

Hagga Neamat, the authentic Egyptian woman who had raised a whole generation on the street, watched the scene with motherly wisdom. On one of those Cairo summer days when the asphalt melts, she decided to fix things between them.

She entered Hassan's shop as he was lighting the fire under the sauce pot. "Remember, my darling, when I taught you the secret of caramelized onions? I told you they must be browned over a low flame. Patience is the key to good taste."

Then she went to Hussein as he was weighing lentils on a digital scale. "Remember, soul of my heart, when I told you the secret of soaking lentils? Exactly six hours, no more, no less."

The brothers froze in place. Hassan left the ladle in the pot, and Hussein stood staring at his mother in astonishment.

"Surprised?" Hagga Neamat smiled. "Come, let's sit in the old Suleiman Pasha coffee shop, and I'll tell you the story from the beginning."

على المقْهى القديمة، تحْت مرْوَحِةْ السّقْف اللي بِتْلِف بِبُطْء، حكِتْلُهُم: "أبوكُم، اللّه يِرْحمُه، كان راجِل عظيم، بسّ كان عنْدُه عيْب واحِد - مكانْش بِيْحِبّ يِشارِك أسْرارُه معَ حدّ. أنا شُفْت فيكُم مِن صُغْرُكُم مَواهِب مُخْتلِفة. إنْتَ يا حسن، كُنْت دايْماً بِتْحِبّ تِجرّب في التَّوابِل و البُهارات. و إنْتَ يا حِسيْن، كُنْت بِتْحِبّ الدِّقّة و النِّظام. فا قرّرْت أطوّر في كُلّ واحِد مَوْهِبْتُه."

خدِت بُقّ مِن الشّاي بِالنّعْناع و كمِّلْت: "الوَصْفة الأصْلية بِتاعِةْ أبوكُم مَوْجودة - بسّ مقْسومة بيْنْكُم. كُلّ واحِد فيكُم عنْدُه نُصّ السِّرّ. إنْتو الاِتْنيْن وَرثِةْ الحاجّ محْمود، و كُلّ واحِد فيكُم بِيْكمِّل التّاني."

الصّمْت لفّ المكان لِلحظات، قطعُه صوْت ضِحْكة مِن حِسيْن: "يَعْني إحْنا زيّ البصْل و الطّماطِم في الصّلْصة - مَيِنْفعوش مِن غير بعْض؟"

"أَوْ زيّ الرُّزّ و المكروْنة!" حسن قال و هُوَّ كمان بِيِضْحك.

دِلْوَقْتي، المحلّيْن بقوا واحِد. حسن مسْؤول عن المطْبخ و التّتْبيلات، و حِسيْن بِيْدير الحِسابات و المقادير. و اليَفْطة الجِديدة بِتْقول:

كُشري الحاجّ محْمود - بِإيد وِلادُه

و تحْتها عِبارة صُغيّرة:

وَصْفِةْ العيْلة... بِتْجمّع مِش بِتِفْرق

و الحاجّة نِعْمات؟ قاعْدة في المحلّ كُلّ يوْم، بِتْراقِب وِلادْها بِفخْر و هُمّا بِيْكمِّلوا مسيرِةْ أبوهُم، و بِتْقول لِلزّبايِن: "سِرّ الكُشري مِش في المقادير... السِّرّ في المحبّة اللي بِتِتْحطّ فيه."

In the ancient coffee shop, under the slowly spinning ceiling fan, she told them, “Your father, may God rest his soul, was a great man, but he had one flaw – he never liked to share his secrets with anyone. I saw different talents in you since you were young. You, Hassan, always loved experimenting with spices and seasonings. And you, Hussein, loved precision and order. So I decided to develop each one’s talent.”

She took a sip of mint tea and continued, “Your father’s original recipe exists – but it’s divided between you. Each of you has half the secret. You are both Hajj Mahmoud’s heirs, and each of you completes the other.”

Silence enveloped the place for moments, broken by Hussein’s laugh. “So we’re like the onions and tomatoes in the sauce – they don’t work without each other?”

“Or like rice and pasta!” added Hassan, also laughing.

Now, the two shops have become one. Hassan is responsible for the kitchen and seasonings, and Hussein manages the accounts and measurements. And the new sign says:

Hajj Mahmoud’s Koshari – By His Sons’ Hands

And underneath, a small phrase:

A Family Recipe... Uniting, Not Dividing

And Hagga Neamat? She sits in the shop every day, proudly watching her sons continue their father’s journey, telling customers, “The secret of koshari isn’t in the ingredients... the secret is in the love you put into it.”

سارة و القُطّة

Sara and the Cat

This story explores the relationship between a young girl and a stray cat in Cairo, where street cats are a familiar part of daily life. In Egyptian cities, cats have maintained a special status since ancient times, freely roaming neighborhoods and often forming bonds with local residents. The tale takes place in one of Cairo's old residential buildings, where a common feature is the perpetually broken أسانْسير *ʔasansər* (elevator) and the بوّاب *bawwāb* (building's doorman) who always promises it will be fixed "tomorrow" – a tomorrow that never comes. These aging buildings, with their long flights of stairs and close-knit community life, form the backdrop for many everyday stories of Egyptian urban life.

Key Vocabulary

- شقّة (*šáʔʔa*) – apartment
- عِمارة (*3imāra*) – apartment building
- سِلِّم (*síllim*) – stairs
- بسْطة (*básṭa*) – landing/platform between flights of stairs
- دوْر (*dōr*) – floor
- بلكوْنة (*balakōna*) – balcony
- حيّ شعْبي (*ђayyə ša3bī*) – popular/working-class neighborhood
- زِيّ المدْرسة (*ziyy ilmadrása*) – school uniform
- فُسْحة (*fúsђa*) – school break time
- الإبْتِدائي (*ilʔibtidāʔī*) – elementary school
- الإعْدادي (*ilʔi3dādī*) – middle school
- صاحْبة أنْتيم (*ṣáђba ʔantīm*) – very close friend
- سنْدَوِتْش (*sandawítš*) – sandwich
- بُكْره (*búkra*) – "tomorrow" (often used in the context of perpetually delayed promises)

A1

Sara and the Cat	*sāra wi -lʔúʈʈa*	سارة و القُطّة
Sara is a little girl.	*sāra bint^{ə} ʂ(u)ɣayyára.*	سارة بِنْت صُغيّرة.
She has a black cat.	*3andáha ʔúʈʈa sōda.*	عنْدها قُطّة سوْدا.
The cat's name is Leila.	*ilʔúʈʈa ʔismáha lēla.*	القُطّة إسْمها ليْلى.
Leila loves Sara.	*lēla bitɦíbb^{ə} sāra.*	ليْلى بِتْحِبّ سارة.
Sara loves Leila.	*sāra bitɦíbb^{ə} lēla.*	سارة بِتْحِبّ ليْلى.
Every day:	*kull^{ə} yōm:*	كُلّ يوْم:
– Sara gives food to Leila	*– sāra bitíddi ʔakl^{ə} l(i)-lēla*	- سارة بِتِدّي أكْل لِليْلى
– Leila eats	*– lēla bitākul*	- ليْلى بِتاكُل
– Leila sleeps with Sara	*– lēla bitnām má3a sāra*	- ليْلى بِتْنام معَ سارة
– Sara is happy	*– sāra mabsūʈa*	- سارة مبْسوطة
Mom and Dad also love Leila.	*māma wi bāba kamān biyɦíbbu lēla.*	ماما و بابا كمان بِيْحِبّوا ليْلى.
The whole family is happy.	*il3ēla kulláha sa3īda.*	العيْلة كُلّها سعيدة.

سارة و القُطّة | Sara and the Cat

كان في بِنْت صُغيّرة إسْمها سارة، عايْشة في شقّة في وِسْط القاهِرة معَ ماما و بابا. كُلّ مرّة بِترْجع مِن المدْرسة، كانِت بِتْشوف قُطّة صُغيّرة سوْدا قاعْدة على السِّلِّم قُدّام شقِّتْهُم.	There was a little girl named Sara who lived in an apartment in central Cairo with her mom and dad. Every time she returned from school, she would see a small black cat sitting on the stairs in front of their apartment.
سارة قالِت: "ماما، عايْزة أجيب القُطّة دي جُوّه البيْت!"	Mom, I want to bring this cat inside! Sara said.
ماما ردِّت: "لأ يا حبيبْتي، مِش مُمْكِن. إحْنا مِش عارْفين القُطّة دي جايّة منيْن."	Mom replied, "No, sweetheart, we can't. We don't know where this cat came from."
لكِن سارة مسِمْعِتْش كلام ماما. في يوْم مِن الأيّام، جابِت شُوَيِّة أكْل لِلْقُطّة و حطِّتْه في طبق صُغيّر. القُطّة كلِت الأكْل كُلُّه و بعْديْن قعدِت جنْب سارة.	But Sara didn't listen to her mom. One day, she brought some food for the cat and put it in a small plate. The cat ate all the food and then sat next to Sara.
و مِن ساعِتْها، كُلّ يوْم سارة كانِت بِتْأكِّل القُطّة. و في الآخِر، ماما و بابا وافْقوا إنُّهم يِخلّوا القُطّة تِعيش معاهُم في البيْت.	From that day on, Sara fed the cat every day. Eventually, Mom and Dad agreed to let the cat live with them in their home.

Sara named the cat “Leila” and they became best friends. Leila would sleep on Sara’s bed every night and would wait for her when she came back from school.	سارة سمِّت القُطّة ”ليْلى“ و بقوا أحْسن صُحاب. ليْلى كانِت بِتْنام على سِرير سارة كُلّ ليْلة، و كانِت بِتِسْتنّاها لمّا تِرْجع مِن المدْرسة.
One day, when Sara was sad because her friend had moved away, Leila sat in her lap and made her laugh.	و في يوْم، لمّا سارة كانِت زعْلانة عشان صاحْبِتْها سافْرِت، ليْلى قعدِت في حُضْنها و خلِّتْها تِضْحك.
Sara said, “See, Mom? Leila is the best gift we’ve ever received!”	سارة قالِت: ”شُفْتي يا ماما؟ ليْلى أحْسن هِدية جتْلِنا!“
Mom smiled and said, “You’re right, sweetheart. Sometimes the best gifts come in the simplest things.”	ماما ابْتسمِت و قالِت: ”معاكي حقّ يا حبيبْتي. ساعات أحْسن الهدايا بِتيجي في أبْسط الحاجات.“
From that day on, Sara learned that love and friendship can come from anywhere, even from a small cat sitting on the stairs.	و مِن يوْمْها، عِرْفِت سارة إنّ الحُبّ و الصّداقة مُمْكِن ييجوا مِن أيّ حِتّة، حتّى لَوْ كانِت قُطّة صُغيّرة قاعْدة على السِّلِّم.

سارة و القُطّة

Sara and the Cat

كان في بِنْت إسْمها سارة، عنْدها اِتْناشر سنة، عايْشة معَ عيْلِتْها في شقّة في عِمارة قديمة في حيّ شعْبي في القاهِرة. الشّقّة في الدّوْر التّالِت، و كان لازِم تِطْلع سِتّين سِلّمة عشان تِوْصل لِبيْتْهُم.

There was a girl named Sara, twelve years old, living with her family in an apartment in an old building in a popular neighborhood in Cairo. The apartment was on the third floor, and she had to climb sixty stairs to reach their home.

كُلّ يوْم بعْد المدْرسة، و هِيَّ طالْعة السِّلِّم الطَّويل ده، كانِت بِتْشوف نفْس المنْظر: قُطّة سوْدا صُغيّرة قاعْدة على البسْطة قُدّام شقِّتْهُم. القُطّة كانِت نحيفة بسّ عيْنيْها كانِت جميلة و بِتِلْمع.

Every day after school, while climbing these long stairs, she would see the same scene: a small black cat sitting on the landing in front of their apartment. The cat was thin but her eyes were beautiful and shiny.

"لَوْ سمحْتي يا ماما!" سارة كانِت بِتِتْحايِل على مامِتْها كُلّ يوْم. "مُمْكِن نِدخّل القُطّة دي عنْدِنا في البيْت؟ شكْلها نضيفة و مُؤدّبة!"

"Oh Mom, please!" Sara would beg her mother every day. "Can we bring this cat into our house? She looks clean and well-behaved!"

ماما ردِّت بِحزْم: "لأ يا حبيبْتي، مَيِنْفعْش. إحْنا مِش عارْفين القُطّة دي جايّة مِنيْن وَلا عنْدها أمْراض وَلّا لأ."

Mom would reply firmly, "No, sweetheart, we can't. We don't know where this cat came from or if she has diseases or not."

لِكِن سارة ما قِدْرِتْش تِقاوِم رغْبِتْها في مُساعْدِةْ القُطّة. في يوْم، خبِّت شُوَيِّةْ فتافيت جِبْنة في جيْب الزِّيّ بِتاعْها، و بعْد المدْرسة، قعدِت تِأكِّل القُطّة بِإيدْها. القُطّة أكلِت بِأدب، و بعْديْن تِتْمسّح في رِجْل سارة و بدأِت تِغمْغِم.

But Sara couldn't resist her desire to help the cat. One day, she hid some cheese crumbs in her uniform pocket, and after school, she sat feeding the cat with her hand. The cat ate politely, then rubbed herself against Sara's leg and started purring.

معَ الوَقْت، بقى فيه روتين يَوْمي: سارة بِتيجي مِن المدْرسة، القُطّة بِتْكون مِسْتنِّياها، و هِيَّ تِأكِّلْها و تِلْعب معاها شُوَيّة. حتّى الأُمّ لاحْظِت إنّ القُطّة نضيفة و مِش بِتْسبِّب أيّ مشاكِل.

With time, there became a daily routine: Sara would come from school, the cat would wait for her, and she would feed her and play with her a little. Even Mom noticed that the cat was clean and didn't cause any problems.

في يوْم حزين، سارة رِجْعِت مِن المدْرسة بِتْعيّط. صاحْبِتْها الأنْتيم هِنْد كانِت لِسّه مِخلّصة آخِر يوْم ليها في المدْرسة عشان عيْلِتْها مِسافْرة كندا. سارة ساعِتْها حسِّت بِالْوَحْدة أَوي.

On a sad day, Sara returned from school crying. Her close friend Hend had just finished her last day at school because her family was moving to Canada. Sara felt very lonely.

لِكِن أوِّل ما فتحِت باب الشّقّة، لِقِت القُطّة مِسْتنِّياها كالْعادة. و كإنّها حسِّت إنّ سارة زعْلانة، فا نطِّت في حُضْنها على طول و فِضْلِت تِغمْغِم و تِتْمسّح فيها لِحدّ ما سارة اِبْتسمِت.

But as soon as she opened the apartment door, she found the cat waiting for her as usual. As if she sensed that Sara was upset, she jumped into her lap immediately and kept purring and rubbing against her until Sara smiled.

فِي اللّحْظة دي، ماما خرجِت مِن المطْبخ و شافِت المنْظر ده. قلْبها رقّ و قالِت: "طيِّب يا سارة، القُطّة بايِن عليْها طيِّبة... مُمْكِن تِدْخُل تِعيش معانا."

At that moment, Mom came out of the kitchen and saw this scene. Her heart softened and she said, "Okay Sara, the cat seems kind... she can come live with us."

سارة فِرْحت أَوي و حضنِت ماما جامِد. سمّوا القُطّة "ليْلى" و جهِّزولْها مكان مخْصوص في البيْت، معَ ذلِك ليْلى كانِت بِتْحِبّ تِنام على سِرير سارة.

Sara was very happy and hugged Mom tightly. They named the cat "Leila" and prepared a special place for her in the house, even though Leila preferred to sleep on Sara's bed.

سارة قالِت و هِيَّ بِتِمْسح على ضهْر ليْلى: "تِعْرفي يا ماما؟ أنا دِلْوَقْتي فِهِمْت إنّ أحْسن الهدايا مُمْكِن تيجي في أبْسط الأشْكال. كُنْت فاكْرة إنّي بساعِد ليْلى، طِلِع هِيَّ اللي ساعْدِتْني."

Sara said, while stroking Leila's back, "You know what, Mom? I now understand that the best gifts can come in the simplest forms. I thought I was helping Leila, it turned out she was the one who helped me."

ماما ابْتسمِت و قالِت: "معاكي حقّ يا حبيبْتي. الحُبّ و الصّداقة مِش مِحْتاجين شُروط."

Mom smiled and said, "You're right, sweetheart. Love and friendship don't need conditions."

سارة و القُطّة

في عِمارة مِن العِمارات القديمة اللي مالْيَة شَوارِع وِسْط البلد في القاهِرة، كانِت عايْشة عيْلة صُغيّرة مُكوّنة مِن أبّ و أُمّ و بِنْتُهُم الوَحيدة سارة، طالِبة في أولى إعْدادي. الشّقّة كانِت في الدّوْر التّالِت، و كان لازِم الواحِد يِتْحمِّل طُلوع السِّلّم الطَّويل عشان يِوْصلّها، خُصوصاً إنّ الأسانْسير بقالُه سِنين مِتْعطّل و البوّاب دايْماً بِيْقول "بُكْره هَيِتْصلّح" معَ إنّ الكُلّ عارِف إنّ "بُكْره" دي مِش هتيجي أبداً.

في يوْم عادي، و سارة راجْعة مِن المدْرسة و شايْلة على ضهْرها شنْطة تِقيلة ملْيانة كُتُب و لابْسة الزِّيّ بِتاعْها المكْوي بِعِنايَة، لفت نظرْها منْظر هَيِفْضل في بالْها طول عُمْرها: قُطّة سوْدا رُفيّعة قاعْدة على بسْطِة السِّلّم قُدّام شقِّتْهُم، عيْنيْها خضْرا و بِتِلْمع و شكْلها يِقطّع القلْب.

سارة كانِت بِتِتْرجّى أُمّها كُلّ ما تِشوف القُطّة: "يا ماما، أرْجوكي! خلّينا نِدخّلْها... واللّه العظيم هاخُد بالي مِنْها و هنضّفْها و أعْمِلّها كُلّ حاجة!"

ماما بِتْحاوِل تِشْرح بِصبْر: "يا بِنْتي، اِفْهمي، مِش مَوْضوع نضافة و بسّ. قُطط الشَّوارِع مُمْكِن تِكون شايْلة أمْراض، و كمان جيران العِمارة هَيِزْعلوا لَوْ عِرْفوا إنِّنا بِنْربّي قُطط."

Sara and the Cat

In one of the old buildings that fill the streets of downtown Cairo lived a small family consisting of a father, mother, and their only daughter, Sara, a student in her first year of middle school. The apartment was on the third floor, and one had to endure the long journey up the stairs to reach it, especially since the elevator had been broken for years, with the doorman would always say "it'll be fixed tomorrow," though everyone knew that "tomorrow" would never come.

On one ordinary day, as Sara was returning from school carrying a heavy bag full of books on her back and wearing her carefully ironed uniform, something caught her eye – a sight that would stay in her memory forever: a thin black cat sitting on the landing in front of their apartment, with bright green eyes and a heartbreaking appearance.

Sara would beg her mother whenever she saw the cat. "Oh Mom, please! Let's bring her in... I swear to God I'll take care of her and clean her and do everything!"

Mom would try to explain patiently. "My daughter, understand, it's not just about cleanliness. Street cats might carry diseases, and also the building's neighbors would be upset if they knew we were keeping cats."

و لكِن زيّ ما بِيْقولوا، القلْب و ما يُريد. سارة مقِدْرِتْش تِقاوِم حنيتْها على القُطّة المِسْكينة. في يوْم ، قرّرِت تِكْسر القَواعِد: خدِت حِتّة مِن السّنْدَوِتْش بِتاع الفُسْحة، و بدل ما تاكْلُه في المدْرسة، خبِّتُه في جيْب الزِّيّ بِتاعْها. أوِّل ما رِجْعِت البيْت، قعدِت تِفتِّت السّنْدَوِتْش لِلْقُطّة اللي كالْعادة كانِت مِسْتنّية على السِّلِم. القُطّة اِتْعامْلِت معَ المَوْقِف بِأدب غريب: أكلِت بِهُدوء، و نضّفِت نفْسها، و بعْديْن قرّبِت مِن سارة و بدأِت تِغمْغِم بِصوْت ناعِم.

معَ مُرور الأيّام، بقى في طُقوس يَوْمية بيْن الاِتْنيْن: سارة تِطْلع مِن المدْرسة بِسُرْعة، قلْبها مشْدود على صاحْبِتْها الجِديدة، و القُطّة مِسْتنِّياها بِكُلّ وَفاء على نفْس البسْطة. حتّى ماما، اللي كانِت في الأوِّل مُعْترِضة جِدّاً، بدأِت تِلاحِظ إنّ القُطّة دي مِش زيّ أيّ قُطّة في شارِع: نضيفة، و مُؤدّبة، و عارْفة حُدودْها.

في نُصّ السّنة الدِّراسية، حصلِت حاجة كسرِت قلْب سارة: هِنْد، صاحْبِتْها الأنْتيم مِن الاِبْتِدائي، جت في يوْم و هِيَّ بِتْعيّط و قالِت إنّ باباها لقى شُغْل في كندا و العيْلة كُلّها هتْسافِر كمان أُسْبوع. سارة رِجْعِت البيْت في اليوْم ده حاسّة إنّ الدُّنْيا اِسْوَدِّت، عيْنيْها ملْيانة دُموع، و قلْبها مَوْجوع على فِراق صاحْبِتْها اللي عُمْرها ما تخيِّلِت إنّها هتِبْعد عنْها.

بسّ اللي حصل بعْد كِده كان غريب: أوِّل ما فتحِت باب الشّقّة، القُطّة السّوْدا نطِّت في حُضْنها على طول، كإنّها حاسّة بِحُزْنها. فِضْلِت تِغمْغم و تِتْمسّح فيها و تِعْمِل حركات لذيفة لِحدّ ما سارة اِبْتسمِت بِرغْم اللي هِيَّ فيه.

But as they say, the heart wants what it wants. Sara couldn't resist her compassion for the poor cat. One day, she decided to break the rules: she took a piece of her break-time sandwich, and instead of eating it at school, hid it in her uniform pocket. As soon as she got home, she sat crumbling the sandwich for the cat who, as usual, was waiting on the stairs. The cat handled the situation with strange politeness: eating quietly, cleaning herself, then approaching Sara and starting to purr softly.

As days passed, daily rituals developed between the two: Sara would rush from school, her heart drawn to her new friend, and the cat would faithfully wait on the same landing. Even Mom, who was very opposed at first, started to notice that this cat wasn't like any street cat: clean, well-mannered, and knew her boundaries.

In the middle of the school year, something happened that broke Sara's heart: Hend, her close friend since elementary school, came one day crying and said that her father had found work in Canada and the whole family would leave in a week. Sara returned home that day feeling like the world had turned black, her eyes full of tears, her heart aching over the separation from her friend whom she never imagined would be far from her.

But what happened next was strange: as soon as she opened the apartment door, the black cat jumped into her lap immediately, as if sensing her sadness. She kept purring and rubbing against her and making sweet movements until Sara, despite herself, smiled.

صادِف إنّ ماما كانِت واقْفة في باب المطْبخ بِتْبُصّ على المشْهد ده، و لِلْمرّة الأولى حسِّت إنّ القُطّة دي مِش مُجرّد قُطّة - دي روْح حِلْوَة جات في وَقْتها. قالِت بِصوْت هادي: "طيِّب يا سارة... القُطّة دي باين عليْها طيِّبة و بِتْحِبِّك... مُمْكِن نجرِّبْها فتْرة تِعيش معانا."

الفرْحة اللي ظهرِت على وِشّ سارة ساعِتْها كانِت أكْبر مِن أيّ كلام. حضنِت أُمّها جامِد و باسِتْها، و على طول اِخْتاروا إسْم "ليْلى" لِلْقُطّة. و جهِّزولْها مكان مخْصوص في البلكوْنة، معَ إنّها في الآخِر كانِت بِتِخْتار سِرير سارة تِنام عليْه.

و في يوْم و هِيَّ قاعْدة بِتْمشّط فرْو ليْلى النّاعِم، سارة قالِت: "تِعْرفي يا ماما؟ أنا دِلْوَقْتي فِهِمْت حاجة مُهِمّة: ساعات أحْلى الهدايا بِتْيجينا مِن غيْر ما نُطْلُبْها، و مِن أماكِن مكُنّاش مُتوَقّعينْها. كُنْت فاكْرة إنّي أنا اللي بساعِد ليْلى، طِلِع إنّها هِيَّ اللي أنْقذِتْني."

ماما ابْتسمِت اِبْتِسامة عميقة و قالِت: "عنْدِك حقّ يا حبيبِةْ قلْبي... في الدُّنْيا دي، أجْمل عِلاقات الحُبّ و الصّداقة هِيَّ اللي بِتيجي كِده، مِن غيْر تخْطيط وَلا شُروط... زيّ ما تِكون نِعْمة ربِّنا بعتْهالْنا في الوَقْت الصّحّ."

It so happened that Mom was standing in the kitchen doorway watching this scene, and for the first time felt that this cat wasn't just a cat – she was a beautiful soul that came at the right time. She said in a quiet voice, "Okay Sara... this cat seems kind and loves you... we can try having her live with us for a while."

The joy that appeared on Sara's face then was beyond words. She hugged her mother tightly and kissed her, and immediately chose the name "Leila" for the cat. They prepared a special place for her on the balcony, though she eventually chose Sara's bed to sleep on.

One day while sitting and brushing Leila's soft fur, Sarah said, "You know what, Mom? I now understand something important: sometimes the best gifts come to us without asking, and from places we didn't expect. I thought I was the one helping Leila, it turned out she was the one who saved me."

Mom smiled a deep smile and said, "You're right, my heart's beloved... in this life, the most beautiful relationships of love and friendship are the ones that come like this, without planning or conditions... like a blessing that God sends at exactly the right time."

هدايا العرايِس

The Brides' Gifts

In the modern district of مدينِةْ نصْر *madīnit naṣr* (Nasr City), where apartment buildings have transformed desert into urban landscape, the ties of community remain strong in Egyptian life. Wedding celebrations, like the one in this story, become events for entire buildings to participate in, particularly during the ليْلِةْ الحِنّة *lēlit ilḫínna* (henna night) – a joyous pre-wedding celebration where the bride's hands and feet are decorated with intricate henna patterns while women sing traditional songs and celebrate together. These communal celebrations are often orchestrated by respected figures like the neighborhood's حاجّة *ḫágga* (hagga) – a maternal figure whose influence extends beyond her own family to all the building's residents. The story also highlights how service workers like عمّ يوسِف *3ammᵊ yūsif* (Uncle Youssef), the delivery man, become integral parts of the community fabric, their daily work weaving them into the neighborhood's social tapestry over decades of delivering life's special moments to people's homes.

Key Vocabulary

- حِنّة (*ɦínna*) – henna (a natural dye for temporary body art)
- عروسة (*3arūsa*) – bride
- فرح (*fáraɦ*) – wedding
- قاعة (*ʔā3a*) – wedding hall
- جِهاز (*gihāz*) – bridal trousseau
- طبْلة (*ţábla*) – traditional drum
- دُفّ (*duff*) – tambourine
- كُوافير (*kuwāfīr*) – hairdresser
- مُغنية (*muɣaníyya*) – female singer
- جلاليب (*galalīb*) – traditional loose dresses
- طرْحة (*ţárɦa*) – headscarf
- جِمّيْز (*gimmēz*) – sycamore tree
- نُقوش (*nuʔūš*) – patterns/designs
- لُمض (*lúmaḑ*) – light bulbs
- بدْلة (*bádla*) – suit

The Brides' Gifts	*hadāya -l3arāyis*	هدايا العرايِس
In a building in Nasr City, there are two brides:	*fi 3imāra f(i) madīnit naṣr, fīha 3arustēn:*	في عِمارة في مدينِةْ نصْر، فيها عروسْتيْن:
– Mona from the third floor	*– múna, ílli fi -ddōr ittālit*	- مُنى اللي في الدّوْر التّالِت
– Noura from the fifth floor	*– nūra, ílli fi -ddōr ilxāmis*	- نورا اللي في الدّوْر الخامِس
The wedding is today.	*ilfárah innahárda.*	الفرح النّهارْده.
The women did henna yesterday.	*issittāt 3ámalu ḥínna ʔimbāriḥ.*	السِّتّات عملوا حِنّة إمْبارِح.
Everyone is happy.	*ilkúllᵊ farḥān.*	الكُلّ فرْحان.
Uncle Youssef brought the gifts:	*3ammᵊ yūsif gāb ilhadāya:*	عمّ يوسِف جاب الهدايا:
– A set of china for Mona	*– ṭaʔmᵊ ṣīni li-múna*	- طقْم صيني لِمُنى
– A chandelier for Noura	*– nágaf li-nūra*	- نجف لِنورا
Uncle Youssef cannot see well.	*3ammᵊ yūsif miš šāyif kuwáyyis.*	عمّ يوسِف مِش شايِف كُوَيِّس.

He mixed up the gifts:	*ɣálaṭ fi -lhadāya:*	غلط في الهدايا:
– He put the chandelier at Mona's	*– ḩaṭṭ innágaf 3andᵊ múna*	- حطّ النّجف عنْد مُنى
– He put the set of china at Noura's	*– ḩaṭṭ iṣṣīni 3andᵊ nūra*	- حطّ الصّيني عنْد نورا
The brides were upset:	*il3arustēn zí3lu:*	العروسْتيْن زِعْلوا:
– Mona wants the china	*– múna 3áyza -ṣṣīni*	- مُنى عايْزة الصّيني
– Noura wants the chandelier	*– nūra 3áyza -nnágaf*	- نورا عايْزة النّجف
The doorman helped:	*ilbawwāb sā3id:*	البوّاب ساعِد:
– He went to the coffee shop	*– rāḩ li-lʔáhwa*	- راح لِلْقهْوَة
– He brought Uncle Youssef	*– gāb 3ammᵊ yūsif*	- جاب عمّ يوسِف
– Uncle Youssef returned the gifts	*– 3ammᵊ yūsif rágga3 ilhadāya*	- عمّ يوسِف رجّع الهدايا
Now at the wedding:	*dilwáʔti fi -lfáraḩ:*	دِلْوَقْتي في الفرح:
– Mona is happy with the china	*– múna mabsūṭa bi-ṣṣīni*	- مُنى مبْسوطة بِالصّيني
– Noura is happy with the chandelier	*– nūra mabsūṭa bi-nnágaf*	- نورا مبْسوطة بِالنّجف

– All people are happy	*– innās kulláha farḫāna*	- النّاس كُلّها فرْحانة
– Uncle Youssef went to buy glasses	*– 3amm^ə yūsif rāḫ yištírī naḍḍāra*	- عمّ يوسِف راح يِشْتِري نضّارة
Thank God, everything became good!	*ilḫámdu li-llāh, kull^ə ḫāga báʔit kuwayyísa!*	الحمْدُ لِلّه، كُلّ حاجة بقِت كُوَيِّسة!

The Brides' Gifts	هدايا العرايِس
In a building in Nasr City, there were two weddings on the same day. Mona from the third floor, and Noura from the fifth floor.	في عِمارة في مدينِةْ نصْر، في فرحيْن في نفْس اليوْم. مُنى اللي في الدّوْر التّالِت، ونورا اللي في الدّوْر الخامِس.
Mona is Doctor Ahmed's bride. Noura is Engineer Hesham's bride. The whole building is happy – two weddings in one day!	مُنى عروسِةْ دُكْتور أحْمد. نورا عروسِةْ البشْمُهنْدِس هِشام. العِمارة كُلّها فرْحانة - فرحيْن في يوْم واحِد!
The day before the wedding, Hagga Souad from the fourth floor did henna for both brides. All the women in the building came down to the garden. They sang and danced and did the henna.	قبْل الفرح بِيوْم، الحاجّة سُعاد اللي في الدّوْر الرّابِع عملِت حِنّة لِلْعروسْتيْن. كُلّ السِّتّات في العِمارة نِزْلوا في الجِنيْنة. غنّوا ورقصوا وعملوا الحِنّة.
On the wedding day, Uncle Youssef the delivery man came with his car. He had many gifts:	في يوْم الفرح، جِهْ عمّ يوسِف بِتاع الدِّليفري بِالْعربية بِتاعْتُه. و معاه هدايا كِتير:
– An expensive set of china for Mona from her aunt	- طقْم صيني فاخِر لِمُنى مِن خالِتْها
– A crystal chandelier for Noura from her aunt	- نجف كْريسْتال لِنورا مِن عمِّتْها

Uncle Youssef was tired and couldn’t see well. He knocked on Mona’s apartment.	عمّ يوسِف تعْبان ومِش شايِف كُوَيِّس. خبّط على شقّةْ مُنى.
“Here you are, bride, your chandelier.”	”اِتْفضّلي يا عروسة، النّجف بِتاعك.“
Then he went to Noura.	وبعْديْن راح لِنورا.
“Here you are, bride, your set of china.”	”اِتْفضّلي يا عروسة، الصّيني بِتاعِك.“
After two hours, Mona opened the gift.	بعْد ساعْتيْن، مُنى فتحِت الهِديه.
“Mom! This is a chandelier! I want the china!”	”يا ماما! ده نجف! أنا عايْزة الصّيني!“
At the same time, Noura screamed:	وفي نفْس الوَقْت، نورا صوّتِت:
“Mom! This is china! I want the chandelier!”	”يا ماما! ده صيني! أنا عايْزة النّجف!“
Mona’s mother quickly went down to Noura’s mother. The doorman ran to look for Uncle Youssef. All the neighbors came down to help.	أُمّ مُنى نِزْلت بِسُرْعة لِأُمّ نورا. البوّاب جِري يِدوّر على عمّ يوسِف. الجيران كُلُّهُم نِزْلوا يِساعْدوا.
Mona’s mother said, “The brides are at the hairdresser, and the wedding is in two hours!”	أُمّ مُنى قالِت: ”العرايِس عنْد الكُوافيْر، والفرح كمان ساعْتيْن!“

Finally, they found Uncle Youssef at the coffee shop. He came back quickly and fixed the gifts.	أخيراً لقوا عمّ يوسِف في القهْوَة. رِجِع بِسُرْعة وظبط الهدايا.
At the wedding:	في الفرح:
– Mona is happy with her set of china	- مُنى فرْحانة بالصّيني بِتاعْها
– Noura is pleased with her chandelier	- نورا مبْسوطة بِالنّجف بِتاعْها
– Everyone is laughing about what happened	- كُلّ النّاس بِتِضْحك على اللي حصل
– And the whole building is celebrating the two brides	- والعِمارة كُلّها بِتِحْتِفِل بِالْعروسْتيْن
Uncle Youssef said, "Thank God! Next time I must wear my glasses!"	عمّ يوسِف قال: "الحمد لِلّه! المرّة الجايّة لازِم ألْبِس النّضّارة!"

هدايا العرايِس

The Brides' Gifts

في عِمارة مِن عِمارات مدينِةْ نصر، الدُّنْيا كُلّها كانِت مشْغولة بِفرحيْن في يوْمِ واحِد. مُنى، مُدرِّسِةْ الإنْجِليزي اللي في الدّوْر التّالِت، هتِتْجوِّز الدُّكْتور أحْمد بِتاع المُسْتشْفى. و نورا، صَيْدلانية اللي في الدّوْر الخامِس، هتِتْجوِّز المُهنْدِس هِشام اللي بِيِشْتغل في شِرْكِةْ بتْروْل.

In one of Nasr City's buildings, everyone was busy with two weddings on the same day. Mona, the English teacher from the third floor, was marrying Doctor Ahmed from the hospital. And Noura, a pharmacist from the fifth floor, was marrying Engineer Hesham who works at an oil company.

العِمارة كُلّها كانِت فرْحانة و بِيْحضّروا لِلْفرحيْن. قبْل الفرحبِأُسْبوع، السِّتّات كُلُّهُم اِجْتمعوا في شقِّةْ الحاجّة سُعاد في الدّوْر الرّابِع عشان يِخطّطوا لِلِيْلِةْ الحِنّة.

The whole building was in a state of joy and preparing for the wedding. A week before the wedding, all the women gathered in Hagga Souad's apartment on the fourth floor to plan the henna night.

الحاجّة سُعاد قالِت: "لازِم نِعْمِلْها في الجِنيْنة! "نِجيب الطّبْلة و الدُّفّ، و نزيِّن المكان بِاللُّمض المِلوِّنة."

Hagga Souad said, "We must have it in the garden! We'll bring the tabla and tambourine, and decorate the place with colored light bulbs."

في لَيْلِةْ الحِنّة، الجِنيْنة اِتْحوِّلِت لِمكان ساحِر. السِّتّات لِبْسوا جلاليب مِلوِّنة، و البنات عملوا زينة حِلْوَة، و الجوّ كان مُبْهِج. مُنى و نورا قعدوا جنْب بعْض، و كُلّ السِّتّات غنّوا:

On henna night, the garden transformed into a magical place. The women wore colored galabeyas, the girls made beautiful decorations, and the atmosphere was festive. Mona and Noura sat next to each other, and all the women sang:

الحنة في إيديكي... و الفرْحة في عِنيْكي...

Henna on your hands... and joy in your eyes...

قبْل الفرح بِيوْم، العِمارة كانِت في حركة مُسْتمِرّة. الهدايا بدأِت تِوْصل لِلْعروسْتيْن. خالِةْ مُنى بعتِت طقْم صيني أصْلي، كامِل بِالشُّوَك و المعالِق و السّكاكين – طقْم لِعِشْرين نفر. و عِمِّةْ نورا بعتِت نجف كْريسْتال تْشيْكي، كِبير و فخْم، بِكْريسْتالات بِتِلْمع و بِتْنوّر الصّالة كُلّها.

The day before the wedding, the building was in constant motion. Gifts started arriving for both brides. Mona's aunt sent a genuine Chinese set, complete with forks, spoons, and knives – a set for twenty people. And Noura's aunt sent a Czech crystal chandelier, large and luxurious, with crystals that sparkle and light up the whole living room.

عمّ يوسِف بِتاع الدِّليفري، اللي بقالُه تلاتين سنة بِيْوَصّل هدايا في المنْطِقة، كان مُرْهق مِن كُتْر المشاوير. نظّارْتُه القديمة مكْسورة، و هُوَّ مِش شايِف كْوَيِّس، بسّ مكْسوف يِقول. وَصل العِمارة السّاعة اِتْنيْن الضُّهْر، و الشّمْس كانِت في عِزّ الحرّ.

Uncle Youssef the delivery man, who had been delivering gifts in the area for thirty years, was exhausted from all his trips. His old glasses were broken, and he couldn't see well, but he was too shy to say so.

He arrived at the building at two in the afternoon, when the sun was at its strongest.

خبّط على شقِّةْ مُنى. فتحِتْلُه أُمّها.

He knocked on Mona's apartment. Her mother opened.

"أهْلاً يا عمّ يوسِف!"

"Welcome, Uncle Youssef!"

"النّجف الكِريسْتال وَصل يا سِتّ الكُلّ. أحُطُّه فيْن؟"

"The crystal chandelier has arrived, madam. Where should I put it?"

"نجف أيْه يا عمّ يوسِف؟ إحْنا مِسْتنِّيين الطّقْم الصّيني!"

"What chandelier, Uncle Youssef? We're waiting for the set of china!"

"أيْوَه أَيْوَه، حاضِر..." قال و هُوَّ مِش واخِد بالُه.

"Yes, yes, of course..." he said, not paying attention.

و في الدّوْر الخامِس، نفْس الحِكايَة اتْكرّرِت معَ نورا. حطّ الصّيني مكان النّجف، و الكُلّ كان مشْغول في التّجْهيزات و محدِّش اِكْتشف الغلْطة.

On the fifth floor, the same story repeated with Noura. He put the china where the chandelier should be, and everyone was too busy with preparations to discover the mistake.

السّاعة أرْبعة العصْر، مُنى رِجْعِت مِن عنْد الكُوافيْر عشان تِغيّر هُدومْها قبْل ما تِروح القاعة. فتحِت الهِدية.

At four in the afternoon, Mona returned from the hairdresser to change her clothes before going to the wedding hall. She opened the gift.

"يا ماما! ده نجف! إحْنا عايْزين الصّيني بِتاعْنا!"

"Mom! This is a chandelier! We want our set of china!"

في نفْس اللّحْظة، صوْت صِريخ نورا كان مسْموع مِن الدّوْر الخامِس: "ده طقْم صيني! فيْن النّجف بِتاعي؟!"

At the same moment, Noura's scream could be heard from the fifth floor. "This is a set of china! Where's my chandelier?!"

البوّاب سِمِع الصُّراخ و طِلِع يِجْري على السِّلِّم. أُمّ مُنى نزْلِت بِسُرْعة، و أُمّ نورا نِزْلِت، و الجيران كُلُّهُم خرجوا مِن شُققْهُم.

The doorman heard the screaming and ran up the stairs. Mona's mother rushed down, Noura's mother came down, and all the neighbors came out of their apartments.

أُمّ مُنى قالِت و هِيَّ مُتوَتِّرة: "العرايِس لازِم يِوْصلوا القاعة السّاعة سبْعة!"

Mona's mother said nervously, "The brides must arrive at the hall by seven!"

أُمّ نورا قالِت كمان: "و العِرْسان مِسْتنِّيين في القاعة!"

Noura's mother added, "And the grooms are waiting at the hall!"

البوّاب لقى رقم عمّ يوسِف في دفْتر التِّليفونات و كلِّمُه. كان قاعِد على القهْوَة بِيِشْرب شاي.

The doorman found Uncle Youssef's number in the phone book and called him. He was sitting at the coffee shop drinking tea.

"اِلْحق يا عمّ يوسِف! الهدايا اِتْلخْبطِت!"

"Hurry, Uncle Youssef! The gifts got mixed up!"

عمّ يوسِف رِجِع بِسُرْعِةْ البرْق. صلّح الغلْطة و اِعْتذر كِتير.

Uncle Youssef came back quick as lightning. He fixed the mistake and apologized profusely.

"سامْحوني يا وِلاد. أصْل النّضّارة مكْسورة..."

"Forgive me, children. You see, my glasses are broken..."

في الآخِر، كُلّ حاجة اِتْظبطِت في الوَقْت المُناسِب.

In the end, everything was fixed just in time.

في قاعة الأفراح:

- مُنى فرْحانة بِالطّقْم الصّيني بِتاعْها
- نورا سعيدة بِالنّجف اللي هَيْزيِّن صالِتْها
- النّاس بِتِحْكي و تِضْحك على اللي حصل
- و العِمارة كُلّها بِتِحْتِفِل بِالْعروسْتيْن الحِلْوين

At the wedding hall:
– Mona is happy with her set of china
– Noura is delighted with the chandelier that will decorate her living room
– People are telling and laughing about what happened
– And the whole building is celebrating the beautiful brides

و عمّ يوسِف؟ في اليوْم التّاني راح اِشْترى نضّارة جِديدة، و كتب على موبايْلُه: خلّي بالك... مُنى: صيني، نورا: نجف!

And Uncle Youssef? The next day he went and bought new glasses, and wrote on his mobile phone: *Remember... Mona: china, Noura: chandelier!*

هدايا العرايِس

في عِمارة قديمة في قلْب مدينِةْ نصْر، مِن المباني اللي شافِت تاريخ الحيّ مِن أيّام ما كان صحرا، كان القدر مِجهِّز مشْهد كوْميدي ظريف. في نفْس اليوْم، في نفْس العِمارة، اِتْصادِف إنّ في عروسْتيْن هَيِتْجوِّزوا - صُدْفة غريبة خلِّت العِمارة كُلّها في حالة طارِئة لِلْفرحيْن.

مُنى، اللي في الدّوْر التّالِت، مُدرِّسِةْ الإنْجِليزي اللي بِتِشْتغل في مدْرسة خاصّة في التّجمّع، هتِتْجوِّز الدُّكْتور أحْمد اِسْتِشاري العظام، قِصِّةْ حُبّ كْلاسيكية بدأِت في عِيادْتُه لمّا راحِت تِكشِّف على رُكْبِتْها. و نورا، الصَّيْدلانية الشّاطْرة اللي في الدّوْر الخامِس، هتِتْجوِّز المُهنْدِس هِشام اللي اِتْعرّفِت عليْه مِن على لينْكْد إن و طِلِع إبْن خالِةْ صاحْبِتْها، مِثال حيّ على إنّ الزّواج قِسْمة و نصيب حتّى في عصْر السّوْشْيال ميدِيا.

الحاجّة سُعاد اللي في الدّوْر الرّابِع، اللي محدِّش في العِمارة بِيِقْدر يِعْمِل مُناسْبة مِن غيْر رأْيَها و بركِتْها، قرّرِت تِتْوَلّى المَوْضوع و تِنظّم ليْلِةْ الحِنّة لِلْعروسْتيْن. "بنات العِمارة زيّ بناتي،" قالِت و هِيَّ ماسْكة التِّليفوْن عشان تِتِّصِل المُغنِّيّات اللي بِيِيجوا يِحْيوا الأفْراح. "لازِم نِعْمِل ليْلة تِتْحِكي."

في الجِنيْنة اللي قُدّام العِمارة، تحْت شجرِةْ الجِمّيْز العتيقة اللي زرعْها بوّاب العِمارة القديم مِن أرْبِعين سنة، اِجْتمعِت كُلّ سِتّات العِمارة. أُمّ وَليد اللي في الدّوْر السّادِس جابِت طبْلة قديمة وارْثاها عن أُمّها، و البنات الصُّغيّرة علّقوا لُمض مِلوِّنة، و الجوّ كان جوّ المصْرِيّين زمان. مُنى و نورا قعدوا جنْب بعْض على كراسي مِتْزيِّنة بِالْوَرْد، و جارِتْهُم المُغنّية المشْهورة في المنْطِقة بدأِت تِغنّي الأغاني التّقْليدية:

The Brides' Gifts

In an ancient building in the heart of Nasr City, one of those buildings that had witnessed the district's history since it was desert, fate was preparing a charming comic scene. On the same day, in the same building, two brides happened to be getting married – a strange coincidence that put the entire building in a state of double-joy emergency.

Mona, from the third floor, the English teacher who works at a private school in El Tagamoa, was marrying Doctor Ahmed, the orthopedic consultant – a classic love story that began in his clinic when she went to check on her knee. And Noura, the clever pharmacist from the fifth floor, was marrying Engineer Hesham whom she met on LinkedIn and who turned out to be her friend's cousin – a living example that marriage is destiny even in the age of social media.

Hagga Souad from the fourth floor, without whose opinion and blessing no one in the building dared hold any occasion, decided to take the initiative and organize the henna night for both brides. "The building's girls are like my daughters," she said while holding her phone to call the traditional singers who enliven weddings. "We must make a night worth telling about."

In the garden in front of the building, under the ancient sycamore tree planted by the old doorman forty years ago, all the building's women gathered. Um Walid from the sixth floor brought an old tabla she inherited from her mother, the young girls hung [strings of] colored light bulbs, and the atmosphere was purely old Egyptian. Mona and Noura sat next to each other on chairs decorated with flowers, and the neighborhood's famous wedding singer began singing traditional songs:

"يا حِنّة يا حِنّة... يا أُمّ الرّنّة و الرّنّة
دُقّوا الطّبول لِلْعروسة... خلّي الفرْحة تِبان عليْها..."

قبْل الفرح بِيوْم، بدأِت الهدايا تِوْصل. خالِةْ مُنى، اللي عايْشة في دُبيّ، بعتِت طقْم صيني فاخِر مُسْتَوْرد - شُغْل صيني أصْلي بِنُقوش دهبية، طقْم كامِل لِعِشْرين نفر، مِن النّوْع اللي السِّتّات بِيِتْباهوا بيه في العُزومات الكِبيرة. و عِمِّةْ نورا، اللي جوْزْها تاجِر نجف في وِسْط البلد، بعتِت نجفة تْشيْكي بِكْريسْتال شفّاف و إضاءة LED حديثة - مزيج بيْن الأصالة و الحداثة، هتْخلّي أيّ صالة تِبان قصْر.

عمّ يوسِف بتاع الدّليفري، إبْن البلد اللي قضّى عُمْره بِيْوَصّل لِلنّاس الفرْحة في بِيوتْهُم، كان في يوْم صعْب. نضّارْتُه القديمة مكْسورة، و المعاش اللي بِياخْدُه مِش مكفّي يِجيب غيْرْها، و كرامْتُه مانْعاهْ يِشْتِكي. في عِزّ الضُّهْر، و الشّمْس ضارْبة في وِشُّه، وَصل العِمارة.

"يا سِتّ الكُلّ، النّجفة وَصلِت، قال لِأُمّ مُنى اللي فتحِتْلُه الباب."

"نجفِةْ أيْه يا عمّ يوسِف؟ إحْنا مِسْتنِّيين الصّيني!"

"أَيْوَه أَيْوَه..." ردّ و هُوَّ بِيِمْسح العرق عن وِشُّه. عيْونُه مِش شايْفة غيْر طشاش.

و في الدّوْر الخامِس، حصل نفْس المَوْقِف معَ عيْلِةْ نورا. و في زحْمِةْ التّجْهيزات لِلْفرح - الفساتين المِتْعلّقة، و الشُّنط الملْيانة مكْياج، و تِليفوْنات الكُوافيْر و المُصوِّرين - محدِّش ركِّز في اللي جُوّه الهدايا.

الكارْثة اُكْتُشِفت السّاعة أرْبعة العصْر، لمّا العروسْتيْن رِجْعوا مِن عنْد الكُوافيْر. الصِّريخْتيْن اللي كانوا في نفْس الوَقْت مِن الدّوْر التّالِت و الخامِس خلّى البوّاب يِفْتِكِر إنّ فيه حريقة.

"Oh henna, oh henna... with your cheerful ring
Beat the drums for the bride... let joy show upon her..."

The day before the wedding, gifts started arriving. Mona's aunt, who lives in Dubai, sent an imported luxury set of china – genuine Chinese work with golden patterns, a complete set for twenty people, the kind women show off at large gatherings. And Noura's aunt, whose husband is a chandelier merchant in downtown, sent a Czech crystal chandelier with clear crystal and modern LED lighting – a blend of authenticity and modernity that would make any living room look like a palace.

Uncle Youssef the delivery man, the son of the country who spent his life delivering people's joys to their homes, was having a difficult day. His old glasses were broken, and his pension wasn't enough to buy new ones, and his dignity prevented him from complaining. At high noon, with the sun hitting his face, he arrived at the building.

"Madam, the chandelier has arrived," he said to Mona's mother who opened the door.

"What chandelier, Uncle Youssef? We're waiting for the china!"

"Yes, yes..." he replied while wiping sweat from his face, his eyes seeing only shadows.

On the fifth floor, the same situation occurred with Noura's family. In the midst of preparations – hanging dresses, bags full of makeup, calls with hairdressers and photographers – no one focused on the contents of the gifts.

The disaster was discovered at four in the afternoon when both brides returned from the hairdresser. The dual scream from the third and fifth floors made the doorman think there was a fire.

"يا خرابي! ده نجف!"

"يا مُصيبْتي! ده صيني!"

في ثَواني، العِمارة كُلّها اِتْحرّكِت. أُمّ مُنى نِزْلِت بِالتّوْب السّاتان بِتاع البيْت، أُمّ نورا نِزْلِت بِالطّرْحة لِسّه في شعْرها، و الجيران خرجوا مِن شُققْهُم زيّ خليةْ نحْل هاجِت. كُلّ واحِد عنْدُه اِقْتِراح:

"نِتّصِل بِالشِّرْكة!"

"نِشوف عمّ يوسِف!"

"نِكلِّم العِرْسان!"

البوّاب، بِخِبْرِةْ سِنين في حلّ مشاكِل العِمارة، عِرِف يِوْصل لِعمّ يوسِف على القهْوَة اللي بِيْقضّي فيها اِسْتِراحِةْ الضُّهْر.

"اِلْحق يا مِعلِّم! الدُّنْيا باظِت!"

عمّ يوسِف، اللي عدّى عُمْرُه كُلُّه بِيْشوف دُموع الفرح في عِيون النّاس، مسْتحْملْش يِكون سبب في حُزْن عروسْتيْن. جِري على العِمارة، طالِع نازِل على السّلالِم بِيْصلّح غلْطِتُه، و اِعْتذر بِمُنْتهى الأدب.

"سامْحوني يا بناتي... عيْني تعْبانة، و المعاش مِش مِكفّي النّضّارة..."

السِّتّات حنّ قلْبُهُم عليْه. أُمّ نورا حطِّت في جيْبُه مبْلغ مُحْترم و بِتْقولُّه: "ده عشان النّضّارة يا عمّ يوسِف."

أُمّ مُنى أصرِّت يِحْضر الفرح: "ده إنْتَ مِن أهْل البيْت."

في قاعِةْ سِنْدِريلّا المُجهّزة لِلْفرحيْن، مُنى بِفُسْتانْها الأوْف وايْت و نورا بِفُسْتانْها الأبْيَض، كانوا أجْمل عروسْتيْن. الهدايا وِصْلِت في مكانْها الصّحّ، و النّاس فِضْلِت طول اللّيْل تِحْكي و تِضْحك على اللي حصل.

"Oh no! This is a chandelier!"

"Oh disaster! This is china!"

In seconds, the whole building mobilized. Mona's mother came down in her house satin top, Noura's mother came down with her scarf still in her hair, and the neighbors emerged from their apartments like a beehive that had been stirred up. Everyone had a suggestion:

"Let's call the company!"

"Let's find Uncle Youssef!"

"Let's call the grooms!"

The doorman, with the wisdom of years of solving building problems, managed to reach Uncle Youssef at the coffee shop where he spent his afternoon break.

"Hurry, master! Everything's gone wrong!"

Uncle Youssef, who had spent his entire life seeing tears of joy in people's eyes, couldn't bear to be the cause of two brides' sadness. He ran to the building, went up and down the stairs, fixed the mistake, and apologized with gentle manners.

"Forgive me, my daughters... my eyes are tired, and the pension isn't enough for glasses..."

The women's hearts softened toward him. Noura's mother slipped a respectable amount into his pocket. "For the glasses, Uncle Youssef."

Mona's mother insisted he attend the wedding. "You're family now."

In the Cinderella Hall prepared for both weddings, Mona in her off-white dress and Noura in her white dress were the most beautiful brides. The gifts reached their correct places, and people spent the whole night telling and laughing about what happened.

عمّ يوسِف قعد في رُكْن بِعيد في الفرح، لابِس بدْلة قديمة نضيفة، و حاطِط على عيْنُه نضّارة جِديدة. اِبْتسم و هُوَّ بِيْتمْتِم: "يا ربّ يِهنّيهُم... و يِخلّيهُم لِبعْض... و يِخلّي مصْر دايْماً فرْحانة بِبناتْها و وِلادْها."

العِمارة القديمة اللي في مدينِةْ نصر شافِت أفْراح كِتير، بسّ المرّة دي كان الفرح مُخْتلِف. مِش بسّ عشان فرحيْن في يوْم واحِد، وَلا عشان حِكايِةْ الهدايا اللي اِتْلخْبطِت... لأ، المرّة دي الفرح كان حِكايَة مصْرية أصيلة عن جيران بقوا أهْل، و غلْطة بسيطة قرّبِت القُلوب أكْتر.

Uncle Youssef sat in a far corner at the wedding, wearing a clean old suit, with new glasses on his eyes. He smiled while mumbling, “May God grant them happiness... keep them for each other... and keep Egypt always joyful with her sons and daughters.”

The old building in Nasr City had seen many weddings, but this time was different. Not just because of two weddings in one day, or because of the mixed-up gifts story... No, this time the wedding was an authentic Egyptian tale about neighbors becoming family, and a simple mistake bringing hearts even closer together.

عِيون سيوَة

The Springs of Siwa

In Egypt's Western Desert lies واحِةْ سيوَة *wāḫit sīwa* (Siwa Oasis), a unique cultural landscape where ancient traditions meet modern tourism. The oasis is known for its distinctive architecture using كرْشيف *karšīf* (karshif) – a building material made from salt rock and mud – and its intricate water management system of عِيون *3iyūn* (natural springs). These springs, which have sustained life in the desert for millennia, are managed through the أفْراج *ʔafrāg* – a traditional system of water channels and irrigation schedules overseen by the community elders. In the B2 version of the story, while fictional spring names are used (following the traditional naming patterns of the Siwi language), they represent the real system where each spring has a traditional name in سيوي *sīwi* (Siwi), the local Amazigh (Berber) language.

Key Vocabulary

- بُحيْرِةْ الملْح (*buɦērit ilmalɦ*) – salt lake
- معْبد آمون (*ma3bad ʔāmūn*) – Temple of Amun
- جبل المَوْتى (*gábal ilmáwta*) – Mountain of the Dead
- حمّام كِليوباتْرا (*ɦammām kiliyubátra*) – Cleopatra's Bath
- عِلاج بِالرّمْل (*3ilāg bi-rráml*) – sand therapy
- مجْلِس (*máglis*) – council
- سِيّاح (*siyyāɦ*) – tourists
- مُرْشِد (*múršid*) – guide
- جَوْلة (*gáwla*) – tour
- صحرا (*ṣáɦara*) – desert
- رِمال (*rimāl*) – sands
- غُروب (*ɣurūb*) – sunset
- خريطة (*xarīṭa*) – map
- تُراث (*turās*) – heritage
- تطوُّر (*taṭáwwur*) – development
- مُناسِب (*munāsib*) – suitable

The Springs of Siwa	***3iyūn sīwa***	**عِيون سيوَة**
Kareem is from Siwa.	*karīm min sīwa.*	كريم مِن سيوَة.
He works as a tour guide.	*biyištáɣal múršid siyāḫi.*	بِيِشْتغل مُرْشِد سِياحي.
He takes tourists to old temples.	*biyāxud issuyyāḫ li-lma3ābid ilʔadīma.*	بِياخُد السُّيّاح لِلْمعابِد القديمة.
Kareem's grandfather knows everything about water.	*gidd^{ə} karīm 3ārif kull^{ə} ḫāga 3an ilmáyya.*	جِدّ كريم عارِف كُلّ حاجة عن المايّة.
Every day he checks the springs in the oasis.	*kull^{ə} yōm biyšūf il3iyūn fi -lwāḫa.*	كُلّ يوْم بِيْشوف العِيون في الواحة.
One day:	*fi yōm:*	في يوْم:
– The water decreased	*– ilmáyya ʔállit*	- المايّة قلِّت
– The palm trees withered	*– innáxl^{ə} díbil*	- النّخْل دِبِل
– The people were sad	*– innās zí3lit*	- النّاس زِعْلِت
Grandfather said, "Come with me, Kareem."	*gidd^{ə} karīm ʔāl: "ta3āla ma3āya ya karīm."*	جِدّ كريم قال: "تعالى معايا يا كريم."
They walked in the oasis.	*mišyu fi -lwāḫa.*	مِشْيوا في الواحة.

They saw all the springs.	*šāfu kúll il3iyūn.*	شافوا كُلّ العِيون.
Grandfather explained:	*gidd^{ə} karīm šáraḫ:*	جِدّ كريم شرح:
– Springs are important	*– il3iyūn muhímma*	- العِيون مُهِمّة
– We must clean them	*– lāzim ninaḍḍáfha*	- لازِم نِنضّفْها
– We must protect them	*– lāzim niḫāfiẓ 3alēha*	- لازِم نِحافِظ عليْها
Kareem understood.	*karīm fíhim.*	كريم فِهِم.
He gathered his friends.	*gámma3 ʔaṣḫābu.*	جمّع أصْحابُه.
They cleaned the springs.	*naḍḍafu -l3iyūn.*	نضّفوا العِيون.
Now:	*dilwáʔti:*	دِلْوَقْتي:
– There is lots of water	*– ilmáyya k(i)tīra*	- المايّة كِتيرة
– The palm trees are green	*– innáxl^{ə} ʔáxḍar*	- النّخْل أخْضر
– The people are happy	*– innās mabsūṭa*	- النّاس مبْسوطة
Kareem tells tourists about water in Siwa.	*karīm biyíḫki li-ssuyyāḫ 3an ilmáyya f(i) sīwa.*	كريم بِيِحْكي لِلسُّيّاح عن المايّة في سيوَة.
Tourists love the story.	*issuyyāḫ biyḫíbbu -lḫikāya.*	السُّيّاح بِيْحِبّوا الحِكايّة.
And Kareem is proud of his homeland.	*wi karīm faxūr bi-báladu.*	و كريم فخور بِبلدُه.

A2

The Springs of Siwa	عِيون سيوَة
Kareem is a young man from Siwa who works as a tour guide. Every day he takes tourists on tours:	كريم شابّ مِن سيوَة، بِيِشْتغل مُرْشِد سِياحي. كُلّ يوْم بِياخُد السُّيّاح في جَوْلات:
– Temple of Amun	– معْبد آمون
– Mountain of the Dead	– جبل المَوْتى
– Salt Lake	– بُحيْرِةْ الملْح
– Cleopatra's Bath	– حمام كِليوباتْرا
Tourists love photos and selfies, and Kareem earns good money from them.	السُّيّاح بِيْحِبّوا الصُّوَر و السّيلْفي، و كريم بِياخُد مِنْهُم فِلوس كُوَيِّسة.
Kareem's grandfather, Uncle Abdullah, is one of the oasis elders. He knows everything about the water springs in Siwa. Every morning he goes to check the spring in their neighborhood.	جِدّ كريم، عمّ عبْدُ اللّه، مِن كُبار الواحة. بِيِعْرف كُلّ حاجة عن عِيون المايّة في سيوَة. كُلّ يوْم الصُّبح بِيْروح يِشوف العيْن اللي في الحيّ بِتاعْهُم.
One day, the spring started to dry up. The water decreased, and the palm trees around the spring began to wither.	في يوْم، العيْن بدأِت تِنْشف. المايّة قلِّت، و النّخيل حَواليْن العيْن بدأ يِدْبل.
"Why did the water decrease, Grandpa?"	"المايّة قلِّت ليْه يا جِدّو؟"

"Come with me, Kareem..."	"تعالى معايا يا كريم..."
His grandfather took him on a walk. They walked through the entire oasis. Uncle Abdullah stopped at each water spring:	جِدُّه خدُه في مِشْوار. مِشْيوا في الواحة كُلّها. عمّ عبْدُ اللّه وِقِف عنْد كُلّ عيْن مايّة:
"All the springs in Siwa are connected underground."	"كُلّ العِيون في سيوَة مِتْوَصّلة معَ بعْض تحْت الأرْض."
"How, Grandpa?"	"إزّاي يا جِدّو؟"
"Our ancestors made a water system hundreds of years ago. We must preserve it."	"أجدادْنا عملوا نِظام لِلْمايّة مِن مِيّات السِّنين. لازِم نِحافِظ عليْه."
Kareem understood that the springs aren't just water. They're the life of the whole oasis.	كريم فِهِم إنّ العِيون مِش مُجرّد مايّة. دي حَياةْ الواحة كُلّها.
Kareem went to the young people in Siwa. He told them about the water problem. Everyone gathered to help:	راح كريم لِلشّباب في سيوَة. قالْهُم عن مُشْكِلةْ المايّة. الكُلّ اِجْتمع يِساعِد:
– They cleaned the springs	- نضّفوا العِيون
– Fixed the old channels	- صلّحوا القنَوات القديمة
– Planted new palm trees	- زرعوا نخيل جِديد

Now, Kareem tells tourists about Siwa's water system:	دِلْوَقْتي، كريم بِيِحْكي لِلسُّيّاح عن نِظام المايّة في سيوَة:
These springs aren't just for photos... they're our life and history.	العِيون دي مِش بسّ لِلصُّوَر... دي حَياتْنا و تاريخْنا.
Tourists listen with interest. And Kareem is proud to tell about his country's heritage.	السُّيّاح بِيْسمّعوا بِاهْتِمام. و كريم فخور إنُّه بِيِحْكي عن تُراث بلدُه.
Uncle Abdullah is happy. He said, "See, Kareem? Siwa isn't just a beautiful place... it's a living story."	عمّ عبْدُ اللّه مبْسوط. قال: "شُفْت يا كريم؟ سيوَة مِش بسّ مكان حِلْو... دي حِكايَة عايْشة."

عِيون سيوَة

The Springs of Siwa

في واحِةْ سيوَة، حيْث النّخيل العالي اللي بِيِحْمي البِيوت الطّينية مِن شمْس الصّحرا، كريم بِيِشْتغل مُرْشِد سِياحي. شابّ في أوائِل العِشْرينات، مُتعلِّم، و عارِف يِتْكلِّم عربي و إنْجِليزي و سيوي.

In Siwa Oasis, where tall palm trees protect mud-brick houses from the desert sun, Kareem works as a tour guide. A young man in his early twenties, educated, and able to speak Arabic, English, and Siwi.

كريم بِياخُد السُّيّاح في جَوْلات يَوْمية: معْبد آمون الشّامِخ، و جبل المَوْتى بِمقابْرُه القديمة، و بُحيْرات الملْح اللي بِتِلْمع في الشّمْس. السُّيّاح بِيْحِبّوا يِتْصوّروا في الأماكِن دي، و بِيِدْفعوا كُوَيِّس.

Kareem takes tourists on daily tours: the lofty Temple of Amun, the Mountain of the Dead with its ancient tombs, and salt lakes that glitter in the sun. Tourists love taking pictures at these places and pay well.

جِدُّه، عمّ عبْدُ اللّه، مِن حُكما الواحة و عارِف أسْرار المايّة في سيوَة. كُلّ يوْم، بِيْلِفّ على العِيون في الحيّ بِتاعْهُم، و بِيْشوف مُسْتَوى المايّة و قُوِّةْ تدفُّقْها.

His grandfather, Uncle Abdullah, is one of the oasis's wise men and knows the secrets of water in Siwa. Every day, he checks the springs in their neighborhood, monitoring water levels and flow strength.

في يوْم مِن أيّام الصّيْف الحارّة، عمّ عبْدُ اللّه لاحِظ إنّ مايِّةْ العيْن الرّئيسية في حيُّهُم قلِّت. النّخيل اللي حَواليْها بدأ يِدْبل، و البساتين بدِأت تِتْأثّر.

On one hot summer day, Uncle Abdullah noticed that water in their neighborhood's main spring had decreased. The surrounding palm trees began to wither, and the gardens started to suffer.

كريم سأل: "المايّة بِتْقِلّ ليْه يا جِدّو؟"

Kareem asked, "Why is the water decreasing, Grandpa?"

"تعالى معايا يا إبْني. لازِم تِتْعلِّم نِظام المايّة في بلدك."

"Come with me, my son. You need to learn your land's water system."

عمّ عبْدُ اللّه و كريم مِشْيوا في دُروب الواحة، مِن عيْن لِعيْن. الجِدّ بِيِشْرح: "كُلّ عيْن في سيوَة ليها دوْر. المايّة بِتِطْلع مِن تحْت الأرْض في أماكِن مُعيّنة، و بعْديْن بِتِجْري في قنَوات قديمة بناها أجْدادْنا."

Uncle Abdullah and Kareem walked through the oasis paths, from spring to spring. The grandfather explained, "Every spring in Siwa has a role. Water emerges from underground at specific points, then flows through ancient channels that our ancestors built."

"و كُلّ بُسْتان لُه يوْم مخْصوص لِلرّيّ." كمِّل عمّ عبْدُ اللّه. "نِظام عادِل وَرِثْناه مِن زمان. لَوْ واحِد مِحْترِمْش دوْرُه، أَوْ قناة اِتْسدِّت، كُلّ الواحة بِتِتْأثّر."

"And each garden has its designated irrigation day," Uncle Abdullah continued. "It's a fair system we inherited from long ago. If someone doesn't respect their turn, or a channel gets blocked, the whole oasis is affected."

كريم بدأ يِفْهم لمّا شاف بِعيْنُه إزّاي البساتين بِتْموت لمّا المايّة تِقِلّ. سأل جِدُّه: "و أيْه الحلّ؟"

Kareem began to understand when he saw with his own eyes how gardens die when water decreases. He asked his grandfather, “What’s the solution?”

الحلّ في إنِّنا نِرْجع نِهْتمّ بِنظام الرّيّ القديم. كُلّ عيْلة مسْؤولة عن جُزْء مِن القنَوات. لازِم نِنضّفْها و نِصلّحْها.

The solution is to return to maintaining the old irrigation system. Each family is responsible for part of the channels. We must clean and repair them.

كريم جمّع شباب الحيّ. شرحْلُهُم المُشْكِلة و إزّاي حَياةْ الواحة كُلّها مُعْتمِدة على المايّة. الشّباب اِتْحمِّسوا لِلْفِكْرة، و بدأوا يِشْتغلوا معَ الكُبار:

Kareem gathered the neighborhood youth. He explained the problem and how the whole oasis’s life depends on water. The young people were excited about the idea and started working with the elders:

- نضّفوا القنَوات مِن الرّمْل و الطّين
- صلّحوا الأماكِن المكْسورة
- رتِّبوا أيّام الرّيّ لِكُلّ بُسْتان
- زرعوا نخيل جِديد حَواليْن العِيون

– They cleaned channels from sand and mud
– They repaired broken sections
– They organized irrigation days for each garden
– They planted new palm trees around springs

معَ الوَقْت، المايّة رِجْعِت تِجْري في القنَوات زيّ زمان. البساتين اِخْضرِّت تاني، و النّخيل رِجِع قَوي.

Over time, water returned to flowing in the channels like before. The gardens turned green again, and the palm trees regained their strength.

كريم غيّر طريقْتُه في الشُّغْل. بدل ما ياخُد السُّيّاح يِتْصوّروا و خلاص، بقى يِحْكيلْهُم عن نِظام المايّة في سيوَة، و إزّاي النّاس عايْشين معَ الصّحرا مِن مِيّات السِّنين.

Kareem changed his way of working. Instead of just taking tourists for photos, he began telling them about Siwa's water system and how people have lived with the desert for hundreds of years.

السُّيّاح اِنْبهروا. واحْدة مِن ألْمانْيا قالِتْلُه: "ده مِش مُجرّد نِظام ريّ... دي حضارة كامْلة!"

Tourists were amazed. A woman from Germany told him, "This isn't just an irrigation system... it's an entire civilization!"

بِاللّيْل، و هُوَّ قاعِد معَ جِدُّه تحْت نخْلة قديمة، كريم قال: "عارِف يا جِدّو؟ كُنْت فاكِر إنّ شُغْل المُرْشِد هُوَّ إنّي أوَرّي السُّيّاح المعابِد و الآثار بسّ. دِلْوَقْتي عِرِفْت إنّ أهمّ حاجة في سيوَة مِش اللي بِنْشوفُه فوْق الأرْض... اللي بِنْشوفُه تحْت الأرْض."

In the evening, sitting with his grandfather under an old palm tree, Kareem said, "You know, Grandpa? I thought a guide's job was just showing tourists temples and ruins. Now I know that the most important thing in Siwa isn't what we see above ground... it's what's below it."

عمّ عبْدُ اللّه اِبْتسم: "وعِرِفْت كمان إنّ المايّة في سيوَة مِش مُجرّد مايّة... دي الحَياة نفْسها."

Uncle Abdullah smiled, "And you also learned that water in Siwa isn't just water... it's life itself."

عِيون سيوَة

في الرُّكْن الغرْبي مِن مصر، حيْث الصّحرا بِتِمْتدّ على قدّ ما العيْن تِقْدر تِشوف، واحِةْ سيوَة بِتْكون عامْلة زيّ لُؤْلُؤة خضرا في بحْر مِن الرِّمال. البِيوت المبْنية بِالْكرْشيف - خليط الطّين و الملْح - بِتِلْمع تحْت شمْس الصّحرا، و النّخيل العالي بِيِرْسِم خطّ السّما.

كريم واحِد مِن شباب سيوَة المِتْعلِّمين، خريج سِياحة و فنادِق، و عارِف يِتْكلِّم عربي و إنْجِليزي بِجانِب اللُّغة السّيوية اللي اِتْعلِّمْها مِن صُغْرُه. بقالُه سنتيْن بِيِشْتغل مُرْشِد سِياحي، بِيْلِفّ بِالسُّيّاح في معْبد آمون و جبل المَوْتى و بُحيْرات الملْح. يِعرّفْهُم على تاريخ المكان، ياخُد معاهُم صُوَر، و يِوَدّيهُم يِجرّبوا العِلاج بِالرّمْل و ياكْلوا التّمْر السّيوي الشّهير.

لِكِن جِدُّه، عمّ عبْدُ اللّه، كان عنْدُه رأْي تاني في السِّياحة و التّطوُّر. "سيوة يا كريم مِش مُجرّد صُوَر و سيلْفي. الواحة دي عايْشة بِنِظام مُحْكم زيّ خليةْ النّحْل، و أهمّ حاجة فيه هِيَّ المايّة."

عمّ عبْدُ اللّه مِن كُبار "مجْلِس سيوَة" التّقْليدي، المسْؤول عن تنْظيم المايّة في الواحة. كُلّ يوْم الصُّبْح، قبْل ما الشّمْس تِطْلع، بِيُخْرُج يِبُصّ على "الأفْراج" - العِيون و القنَوات اللي بِتِسْقي بساتين النّخيل و الزّيْتون.

في يوْم صيْفي و الجوّ حرّ أَوي، عمّ عبْدُ اللّه لاحِظ إنّ عيْن "تغْرفْت" - مِن أهمّ عِيون الحيّ - بدأِت تِنْشف. النّخْل اللي حَواليْها بدأ يِدْبل، و النّاس بدأِت تِشْتِكي مِن قِلِّةْ المايّة.

The Springs of Siwa

In Egypt's western corner, where desert extends until the eye tires, Siwa Oasis lies like a green pearl in a sea of sand. Houses built with karshif – a mixture of mud and salt – glisten under the desert sun, and tall palm trees draw the skyline.

Kareem is one of Siwa's educated youth, a tourism and hospitality graduate who speaks Arabic and English alongside the Siwi language he learned in childhood. For two years, he's worked as a tour guide, taking tourists around the Temple of Amun, the Mountain of the Dead, and the salt lakes. He introduces them to the place's history, takes photos with them, and takes them to try sand therapy and taste Siwa's famous dates.

But his grandfather, Uncle Abdullah, had a different view of tourism and development. "Siwa, Kareem, isn't just about photos and selfies. This oasis lives by an intricate system like a beehive, and its most important element is water."

Uncle Abdullah is one of the elders of the traditional "Siwa Council," responsible for organizing water in the oasis. Every morning, before sunrise, he goes out to inspect the "afrag" – the springs and channels that irrigate the palm and olive groves.

On an intensely hot summer day, Uncle Abdullah noticed that "Taghraft" spring – one of the neighborhood's most important springs – was starting to dry up. The surrounding palm trees began to wither, and people started complaining about water scarcity.

نادى على حفيدُه: "تعالى يا كريم. لازِم تِفْهم سِرّ المايّة في سيوَة."

أخد جِدُّه يِمْشي في دُروب الواحه، و معَ كُلّ خطْوَة كان بِيِحْكي قِصّة: "كُلّ عيْن في سيوَة ليها إسْم و أصْل. تِعْرفْت دي مُتّصِلة تحْت الأرْض بِعيْن تاقْزال و عيْن تامْراقي. أجْدادْنا فِهْموا الوَصْلة دي، و عملوا نِظام مُحْكم: كُلّ بُسْتان لُه يوْمُه المعْروف في السّقْي، و كُلّ عيْلة مسْؤولة عن تنْضيف جُزْء مِن القنَوات."

كريم كان بِيِسْمع و هُوَّ مِش مِصدّق. سنتيْن بِيِشْتغل في سيوَة و أوِّل مرّة يِعْرف الكلام ده. "وليْه المايّة بِتْقِلّ دِلْوَقْتي يا جِدّو؟"

عشان نِسينا النِّظام القديم. النّاس مشْغولة بالسِّياحة و الفنادِق، و القنَوات ملْيانة رمْل، و العِيون بِتِضْعف.

في البيْت، قعد كريم يِدوّر على النِّت. و اِكْتشف إنّ نِظام المايّة في سيوَة مِش مَوْجود في كُتُب السِّياحة، معَ إنُّه مِن أقْدم و أدقّ نُظُم الرّيّ في العالم. حسّ بِالذّنْب - إزّاي يِكون مُرْشِد في بلدُه و مَيِعْرفْش الحاجات دي؟

جمّع شباب الحيّ و حكالْهُم اللي عِرْفُه. في البِدايَة، بعْضُهُم شاف إنّ المَوْضوع قديم و ملوش لازْمة. لكِن لمّا البساتين بدأِت تِموت و النّخْل يِدْبل، فِهْموا إنّ المُشْكِلة بِجدّ.

بِمُساعْدِةْ الكُبار في المجْلِس، الشّباب بدأوا شُغْل مُنظّم:

- رسموا خريطة لِكُلّ العِيون و القنَوات في الحيّ
- نضّفوا "الأفْراج" مِن الرّمْل و الطّين
- صلّحوا القنَوات المكْسورة
- رتِّبوا جدْوَل جِديد لِلرّيّ يِناسِب الوَضْع الحالي

He called his grandson, "Come, Kareem! You need to understand the secret of water in Siwa."

His grandfather took him walking through the oasis paths, telling a story with every step, "Every spring in Siwa has a name and a lineage. Taghraft is connected underground to Tagzal spring and Tamraqi spring. Our ancestors understood this connection and created a precise system: each garden has its known irrigation day, and each family is responsible for cleaning part of the channels."

Kareem listened in disbelief. Two years working in Siwa and this was the first time he'd learned this. "Why is the water decreasing now, Grandpa?"

Because we've forgotten the old system. People are busy with tourism and hotels, the channels are full of sand, and the springs are weakening.

At home, Kareem researched on the internet. He discovered that Siwa's water system isn't mentioned in tourism books, despite being one of the world's oldest and most precise irrigation systems. He felt guilty – how could he be a guide in his homeland without knowing these things?

He gathered the neighborhood youth and told them what he'd learned. At first, some saw it as outdated and unnecessary. But when gardens started dying and palm trees withering, they understood the problem was serious.

With help from the council elders, the young people began organized work:
– They mapped all springs and channels in the neighborhood
– They cleaned the "afrag" of sand and mud
– They repaired broken channels
– They arranged a new irrigation schedule suitable for current conditions

مَعَ الوَقْت، المايّة رِجْعِت تِجْري في القنَوات. البساتين اِخْضرِّت، و النّخيل اِسْتعاد قُوِّتُه. لكِن الأهمّ مِن كِده، إنّ كريم اِكْتشف طريقة جِديدة في شُغْلُه.

بدل ما ياخُد السُّيّاح في جَوْلة سريعة، بقى بِياخُدْهُم في "رِحْلِةْ المايّة في سيوَة". بِيْوَرّيهُم إزّاي النّاس عاشوا في الصّحرا آلاف السِّنين، و إزّاي العِيون و القنَوات خلِّت الحَياة مُمْكِنة في قلْب الصّحرا.

السُّيّاح اِنْبهروا. الصُّوَر اِتْحوِّلت مِن مُجرّد سيلْفي قُدّام المعابِد، لِصُوَر بِتِحْكي قِصِّةْ حضارة كامْلة. و كريم نفْسُه بقى يِشوف بلدُه بِعيْن جِديدة.

"تِعْرف يا جِدّو؟" قال لِجِدُّه و هُمّا قاعْدين تحْت نخْلة قديمة في الغُروب. "كُلّ ما أعْرف حاجة عن سيوَة، بحِسّ إنّ فيه حاجات تانْيَة كِتير لِسّه مِحْتاج أتْعلِّمْها."

عمّ عبْدُ اللّه اِبْتسم: "سيوَة زيّ العيْن يا كريم... كُلّ ما تُحْفُر فيها، تِلاقي مايّة جِديدة."

Over time, water returned to flowing in the channels. Gardens turned green, and palm trees regained their strength. But more importantly, Kareem discovered a new way of doing his job.

Instead of taking tourists on quick tours, he began taking them on "Siwa's Water Journey." He shows them how people have lived in the desert for thousands of years, and how springs and channels made life possible in the heart of the desert.

Tourists were amazed. Photos transformed from mere selfies in front of temples to pictures telling the story of an entire civilization. And Kareem himself began to see his homeland through new eyes.

"You know, Grandpa?" he said to his grandfather as they sat under an old palm tree at sunset. "The more I learn about Siwa, the more I feel there are many things I still need to learn."

Uncle Abdullah smiled, "Siwa is like a spring, Kareem... the more you dig, the more water you find."

www.ingramcontent.com/pod-product-compliance
Lightning Source LLC
Chambersburg PA
CBHW071524120626
46550CB00006B/2356
9781962752046